Beyond Muesli and Fondue
The Swiss Contribution to Culinary History

Beyond Muesli and Fondue

The Swiss Contribution
to Culinary History

Martin Dahinden

CONTENTS

PREFACE

The saying „Dining is the life and soul of diplomacy" comes from Lord Palmerstone, the British prime minister who also served as foreign minister three times. That does not mean that diplomacy is primarily about dining, but that diplomats themselves are still at work while they are dining and therefore those official dinners are far more than events of secondary importance in diplomacy.

In the diplomatic world, official dinners are important for two different reasons. They provide a framework for the exchange of information and opinions, for communication, for negotiations, but also for personal contacts. Official dinners, receptions, and cocktail receptions allow diplomats to hear about facts and to make statements which would hardly be possible at conferences or meetings. Great diplomats like Metternich and Talleyrand were masters at the art of switching between different frameworks and using them for political purposes. Even two hundred years later, under completely different political and cultural conditions, official dinners and receptions have kept that traditional task, from carefully orchestrated state visits to the daily work of diplomats, which is managed without much glamour and with little public interest.

But official dinners not only provide a framework for exchanges. The dishes and the way they are presented and served express contents themselves. In other words: culinary art is a form of communication through which states, but also other institutions, present themselves and convey messages. This second role of dining culture in diplomacy can also be traced far back to antiquity.

Before my wife Anita and I came to Washington in 2014 and assumed our role as an ambassadorial couple, we asked ourselves the question, "How do we want to portray Switzerland from the culinary standpoint at the countless events at the Swiss Residence in the United States?" There is nothing wrong with our country's simple dishes. Bratwurst, Raclette, Fondue, Birchermüesli and Rösti are firmly established and are expressive political symbols. But do they reflect Switzerland with its excellent gastronomy, the country with the most *Michelin Guide* stars per capita and our important contributions to culinary history? Do they draw attention to what Switzerland is: one of the most innovative and global countries in the world with a strong economy and a worldwide presence through its quality products and well-known brands?

Since we could not find any book that suited our purpose, I went in search of stories and anecdotes about dishes, chefs, bakers, and gastronomes. It was an exciting and productive search. I came upon the story of the most important chef of the Renaissance, who came from Ticino, the first woman who ever wrote a cookbook, the tragic fate of a man who arranged splendid banquets for the Sun King, and pioneers of the hotel business and of industrial food production. I found out about Napoleon's chef, the founders of the legendary Delmonico's Restaurant in New York, a revolutionary who wrote a monumental culinary dictionary and began to organize his colleagues into groups throughout the world. I found out how Swiss confectioners and chocolate producers made a name for themselves abroad, that a Swiss man ran the first American Bar in Europe, and a resourceful mind from Ticino invented the ice cream cone. In Washington, I met a Swiss Executive Chef who worked for five American presidents in the White House.

Swiss cuisine is rich in anecdotes which connect the country's political history with its culinary history and say a great deal about the characteristic features of Switzerland. The result of my research, a volume with brief stories and original recipes, was published in German as *Schweizer Küchengeheimnisse* in 2016 and brought me many appearances and much attention in the Swiss media.

But what was most important were the many events at the Swiss Residence in Washington which served as the stage for those stories and dishes. American guests immediately found them interesting and they also became a local conversation topic. Individual dinners were devoted to great Swiss chefs with recipes from their time, from the Renaissance, through the Baroque, Empire and Belle Époque periods to the present day. Events were underpinned with culinary creations, for example, the event on the opening of the new Gotthard Base Tunnel, the presentation of the Tell Award to Claude Nicollier, the only Swiss astronaut up to now, and events promoting the Festival del film Locarno and the Montreux Jazz

Festival, occasion when we hosted George Lazenby, the one-time James Bond from *On Her Majesty's Secret Service*, and at many lunches and dinners for American guests.

Why are events and their messages so much more effective if they are reinforced by culinary creations? The answer is simple: because eating and drinking appeal to all the senses at the same time.

A number of people assisted me in writing this book. I would like to thank my wife, Anita, for her interest and her critical comments. I would also like to thank all my colleagues at the Embassy of Switzerland in Washington, especially the team at the Residence, who made successful events possible with their great commitment.

Joao Marcos Barboza, the masterful chef of the Swiss Residence, transformed old recipes into modern recipes based on the same ingredients and with the same flavors as the original ones. Most of the recipes in this book were rewritten and adapted by him.

My heartfelt thanks go to Cheryl A. Fain, the Embassy of Switzerland's official translator, who demonstrated great expertise and cultural knowledge in her precise and careful German-into-English translation and editing of this book.

Interns from the world of gastronomy contributed to individual chapters and brought culinary Switzerland closer to the American public through events. I am grateful to Manuela Flattich (Ice Cream), Nicolas Roth Macedo (Cocktails), Jana Schneuwly (Desserts), and Aline Flückiger (Soups).

Unlike S*chweizer Küchengeheimnisse, Beyond Muesli and Fondue* is not a nonfiction book with stories, but a cookbook with cultural history texts which invites readers to follow the recipes. The eyes, nose, palate, and stomach are invited to go on an exploration trip while taking a journey through time.

Martin Dahinden

SUNLIGHT FOOD:
DR. BIRCHER-BENNER
AND HIS MUESLI

Müesli or *Birchermüesli* is the most famous Swiss food. You can find it everywhere now, in shops and at breakfast tables. This healthy dish is newer than many would expect. It has a troubled history and only a few people know the original recipe.

Life reform movements came into being in Germany, Austria and Switzerland from the second half of the nineteenth century. Their starting point was criticism of modern lifestyles, the consequences of industrialization, urbanization and other passing fads.

The life reform movements were not a uniform phenomenon, but had very different ideological backgrounds and social characteristics. Some of them were progressive; many of them were truly reactionary and even racist. Others, though, were simply bizarre. The enthusiasm for reform encompassed very different areas of life.

In their criticism of the modern age, many life-reform adherents sought lifestyles close to nature to avoid the impact of societal change. Therefore they turned to organic farming, natural medicine, and nudism; some began to wear natural-style clothes made from natural fabrics; they tested new types of settlements and living arrangements such as the inhabitants of the Monte Verità colony in Ticino and of rural communes. Parts of the life reform movement cultivated new religious and spiritual practices. Primarily, but not exclusively, members of the upper class underwent self-realization in the life reform movement. The widespread skepticism toward the scientific and economic establishment gave laymen a big role. Women, who had few public rights in society at that time, played a considerable role in the life reform movement.

Sanatoriums and *Naturheilanstalten* were part of the new understanding of nature and the human body. Already in 1853, the Swiss Arnold Rikli opened a sun sanatorium, where he prescribed "light baths" in the nude for his patients. In doing so, he became a forerunner of nudism. Many supporters of the life reform movement were fascinated by primordial life and by the still unspoiled natural beauty in Switzerland. The country with the wild mountain landscape had a special attraction for many.

Nutrition was one of the most important fields of activity of the life-reform adherents. In the second half of the nineteenth century, the modernization of the food industry and falling prices for agricultural products such as sugar and white flour led to fundamental changes in nutritional habits. Preserved food and ready-to-serve products came onto the market at the same time. Many nutritional reformers considered the nutritional changes to be the cause of the poor state of health of the population. They were of the opinion that only natural food was truly healthy, that is, raw fruit and vegetables, milk and wholegrain products. With that, they were in opposition to the predominant dietetics, which regarded animal protein as the most important energy supplier for the human body. The familiar name *Reformhaus* used for grocery stores with natural products goes back to the time of the life reform movements.

The Swiss doctor Maximilian Oskar Bircher-Benner, who lived from 1867 to 1939, was an excellent exponent of nutritional reform. As a young man, he had a doctor's practice in Zurich's industrial quarter, where he was exposed to the poor state of health of many working-class families. Later on, though, he discovered that well-to-do people on the posh Zürichberg were also undernourished and their state of health left a great deal to be desired. Bircher-Benner was convinced that nutrition alone could be the cause of the poor state of health.

Like many of his contemporaries in reform movements, he associated his ideas about nutritional reform with philosophical ideas. He believed that sunbeams represented a cosmic force flowing through each living thing, thus maintaining the biological order. Plants receive this vital force the most directly. Human beings and animals obtain it indirectly from food. Bircher-Benner was convinced that this vital energy is contained in its purest form in raw fruit and vegetables.

His ideas met with opposition. The Zurich medical profession rejected Bircher-Benner's ideas as unscientific and began to ostracize him. The farmers' association, which was interested in livestock breeding from the economic standpoint, also pulled him to pieces. In defending his dietetics, Bircher-Benner referred to the eating habits of the citizens of the Old Swiss Confederation and to the culture of mountain farmers. Their daily diet was very simple, often only consisting of a single dish. A part of that daily diet included porridge made from oats, millet and barley, with the addition of an herb (especially beet and cabbage), turnips and other root vegetables, beans, fresh milk as well as fresh and dried fruit. Meat was served only occasionally, however. What Bircher-Benner had actually described were the rustic eating habits of the Middle Ages, which had been preserved in many Swiss mountain valleys up to the age of industrialization.

Despite the disparagement and hostility he encountered, Dr. Bircher-Benner did not let himself be swayed and held to his theory of sunlight food. In 1904, he opened a sanatorium with the programmatic name *Lebendige Kraft* (Vital Force) on the Zürichberg. In addition to healthy food, the sanatorium offered outdoor activities, air baths, hydrotherapy and physical exercises. Bircher-Benner saw his sanatorium as a workshop against degeneration through unnatural lifestyles. *Lebendige Kraft* was not a wellness zone, however. Whoever underwent the treatment got into a rigorous program with little leeway. Thomas Mann, who was a patient at Bircher-Benner's and also found the inspiration for his famous novel *Der Zauberberg* (*The Magic Mountain*) at the sanatorium, described Bircher-Benner's clinic as a "hygienic prison" in a letter. Nevertheless the clinic attracted many prominent personalities including Rainer Maria Rilke, Hermann Hesse, Wilhelm Furtwängler and Yehudi Menuhin.

Through *Bircher-Müesli*, which is named after him, he secured lasting posthumous fame. In its original form, *Bircher-Müesli* was prepared from rolled oats, water, apples (grated with skin and core), lemon juice and sweetened condensed milk, sprinkled with ground nuts and almonds at the end. It was important to Dr. Bircher-Benner that muesli be prepared immediately before the meal. At his clinic, the dish was served as breakfast or supper, sometimes also as a first course at lunch; however, not as a complete meal or a dessert. Dr. Bircher-Benner followed a strict recipe for his muesli. Today there are no longer any fixed rules. All sorts of similar dishes are now called muesli or Bircher muesli. Together with Swiss chocolate and cheese fondue, it is the most widespread dish from Switzerland throughout the world.

BIRCHERMÜESLI
D'Spys / Die Speise

Ingredients: Soak 1 spoonful of rolled oats in 3 spoonful of water for 12 hours; 1-2 apples with skin and core, remove stem and bud; 1 spoonful ground tree nuts, hazelnuts and almonds; 1 spoonful sweetened condensed milk; honey or sugar; juice from half of a lemon.

Preparation: Mix rolled oats with the water, condensed milk and lemon juice shortly before the meal; grate in apples with a Bircher grater. Immediately mix everything together and serve.

Original recipe according to Dr. Maximilian Oskar Bircher-Benner

A Chocolate Dinner

Mountains, watches, cheese, and chocolate are immediately associated with Switzerland. However, chocolate was not even invented by the Swiss. More than two-and-a-half thousand years ago, the Mayans cultivated cacao trees, and their language gave us the name *xocolatl* for a beverage made from cocoa beans. In the 16th century, Spanish conquerors brought cocoa to Europe, where the strangely bitter drinking chocolate became a popular drink among the aristocracy. In the salons toward the end of the *ancien régime*, however, drinking chocolate was replaced by coffee and tea. Nevertheless, the triumph of edible chocolate first began at fairs in Italy and soon through industrial production.

Besides the old tradition of pastry and cake making, there was little hint of a successful chocolate industry in Switzerland. The main raw materials, cocoa and sugar, had to be imported. Yet the Swiss chocolate manufacturers successfully followed a strategy similar to that of the watchmakers: they focused on quality, innovation, and high added value. Chocolate production did not originate as a bold industrial design, but as typically Swiss by craftsmanship and attention to detail.

François-Louis Cailler opened a chocolate factory near Vevey in 1819; he was quickly followed by other pioneers whose names are still famous today: Philippe Suchard, Jacques Foulquier (Favarger), Rudolf Sprüngli, Aquilino Maestrani, Johann Georg Munz, Rodolphe Lindt, Jean Tobler, and Max Frey.

In the 19th century, Swiss chocolate production was strongly geared toward exports. Its heyday was the *Belle Époque*. At that time, Swiss chocolate manufacturers increased their share of the world market to over fifty percent. Their success story is closely linked to the upturn in tourism. After World War II, the strategy changed. Swiss chocolate manufacturers increasingly invested abroad and began to produce chocolate adapted to local tastes. Switzerland itself has remained an important market: in chocolate consumption, Swiss people always rank among the top chocolate lovers in the world.

Chocolate is more than a sweet. One of the popular dinners at the Swiss Residence in Washington is the "Chocolate Dinner," which features chocolate in every course and became a topic of social conversation in Washington. The recipes of this remarkable menu are by Chef Marcos Barboza of the Swiss Residence.

CHOCOLATE FOIE GRAS MOUSSE TRUFFLES

Salt-Spiced Dark Chocolate and Curry White Chocolate Foie Gras Mousse Truffles, Candied Bacon, Brioche Croutons, Spiced Blackberry Chutney, Pistachios.

Serves 4

> *7 oz. foie gras mousse, good quality*
> *4 oz. white chocolate, melted*
> *4 oz. dark chocolate, melted*
> *1 teaspoon curry powder*
> *1 teaspoon chili powder*
> *⅛ teaspoon cayenne pepper*
> *Salt and pepper*
> *2 tablespoons pistachios*
> *8 fresh blackberries, cut in half*
> *Candied Bacon (recipe follows)*
> *Spiced Blackberry Chutney (recipe follows)*
> *8 round brioche croutons, a bit bigger than the size of the foie gras balls*

Start by softening the foie gras mousse, leaving it out at room temperature, then lightly whipping it with a mixer with a paddle attachment on medium low speed (do not overwhip it or the mousse will break).

Using a small ice cream scoop, scoop out eight perfectly shaped balls of the foie gras mousse and set on a parchment paper-lined tray and place in the freezer until it is hardened.

Meanwhile, melt both white and dark chocolate separately by placing them in separate bowls that are set on top of a double boiler on low heat, and let them melt slowly without stirring. Then remove the bowls from the heat and, using a rubber spatula, stir the white and the dark chocolate very delicately until they are nicely melted and shiny.

Add the curry powder to the white chocolate and stir to combine and season with salt and pepper to taste.

Add the chili powder and cayenne pepper to the dark chocolate and stir to combine and season with salt and pepper to taste.

Remove the foie gras balls from the freezer and, using a thin bamboo skewer to insert into the foie gras balls, dip four balls into the melted white chocolate and four into the melted dark chocolate, and cover all sides with the chocolate, then shake it gently to get rid of excess chocolate, leaving a nice and thin covering and then place them on a parchment paper-lined tray and put them in the refrigerator.

CANDIED BACON

> *2 thick slices of smoked bacon, cut into 4 equal pieces*
> *½ cup sugar*
> *1 teaspoon water*

Crisp the bacon pieces on both sides in a frying pan without adding any oil. Remove from the pan and drain on paper towels. Set aside.

Put the sugar into a small saucepan and add the water and mix to make a paste. Cook the sugar on low heat without stirring until a caramel is formed with a nice amber color (be careful not to overcook it and burn the sugar).

Remove the pan from the heat and immediately add the crispy bacon pieces and stir into the caramel to nicely cover all the bacon pieces. Remove the bacon from the caramel and place the pieces on a parchment paper-lined tray 2 inches apart and let them harden. Keep aside.

SPICED BLACKBERRY CHUTNEY

> *1 cup fresh blackberries*
> *1 tablespoon olive oil*
> *¼ cup red onions, diced*
> *½ teaspoon fresh ginger, grated*
> *1 cinnamon stick*
> *1 star anise*
> *¼ teaspoon freshly ground black peppercorn*
> *2 teaspoons balsamic vinegar*
> *1 tablespoon brown sugar*
> *¼ teaspoon salt*

Heat the oil in a saucepan on medium heat. Add the onions and let them cook for 3 to 5 minutes until they are soft.

Add all the other ingredients and stir and let it all simmer for 20 to 30 minutes, stirring frequently and breaking up the blackberries.

Remove the cinnamon stick and the star anise and process the chutney in a food processor until smooth. Transfer the mixture to a small squeeze bottle and place it in the refrigerator until ready to use.

Assembly:

Separate four nice white plates, and on each plate put two brioche croutons side by side 3 inches apart. Place the chocolate-covered foie gras truffles, one of each color, on top of the croutons. Place one piece of the candied bacon on top of each foie gras truffle and one pistachio on top of each bacon piece.

Make dots of the chutney around the plates with the squeeze bottle filled with the blackberry chutney. Divide the fresh blackberries equally among the plates and scatter a few pistachios around the plates. You can add some fresh green herbs or micro greens here and there to add some color to the presentation.

CHOCOLATE FETTUCCINI

Serves 4

PASTA DOUGH

> *2 cups cake flour*
> *¾ cup all-purpose flour*
> *¼ cup cocoa powder*
> *⅛ teaspoon salt*
> *4 large egg yolks, at room temperature*
> *¼ cup extra virgin olive oil*

Place the cake flour, all-purpose flour, cocoa powder, salt and egg yolks in a food processor. Pulse to combine. With the machine running, gradually add the oil, and then a third to a half cup of water until the mixture forms a dough (the dough should stick together if pinched between your fingers). If necessary, add additional water, 1 teaspoon at a time, if the dough is too dry.

Place the dough on a lightly floured surface. Gather the dough into a ball and knead until smooth, about 5 minutes. Cover with plastic wrap and refrigerate for 30 minutes.

Cut the dough into quarters and press flat. Run each piece of pasta dough several times through a pasta-rolling machine, adjusting the setting each time until the pasta is about one-eighth to one-sixteenth of an inch thick. Cut the pasta into fettuccine noodles. Coat the cut pasta with cocoa powder to prevent sticking.

CAPER, BLACK OLIVES, SUN DRIED TOMATOES, AND PEPPERONCINO SAUCE

> *1 small shallot, finely diced*
> *⅛ cup capers, chopped*
> *¼ cup kalamata olives, chopped*
> *¼ cup sun dried tomatoes, chopped*
> *½ teaspoon pepperoncino chili flakes*
> *1 tablespoon extra virgin olive oil*
> *2 tablespoons fresh parsley, finely chopped*
> *Salt and pepper*

Fill a large pot with salted water and bring to a boil on high heat.

In a large nonstick frying pan, on medium heat, cook the shallots in olive oil until soft, then add all the other ingredients except for the parsley. Season with salt and pepper to taste (keep in mind that the capers and olives are already salty) and cook for 5 minutes.

Meanwhile, add the pasta to the boiling water and cook until tender but firm to the bite, stirring occasionally, 2 to 3 minutes. Drain the pasta and add the pasta to the sauce. Add the fresh chopped parsley and, using a pair of tongs, mix all together to combine. Serve at once.

Coconut Water and Cocoa Nibs Granité

Serves 4

> 4 cups coconut water
> 1 tablespoon finely chopped cocoa nibs
> 2 tablespoons honey

Pour the coconut water into a bowl. Add the honey and stir to dissolve. Add the cocoa nibs.

Pour the mixture into a glass 8 x 8-inch pan. Carefully place it uncovered in the freezer for 4 to 5 hours. Remove the pan every 2 hours and scrape the ice with a fork and place it back in the freezer. Repeat this process until you have a granité of snow-like consistency. Keep it frozen and, just before serving, scrape it one more time and scoop into sherbet glasses and serve.

Chocolate, Coffee, and Chipotle Braised Beef Short Ribs with Fried Polenta and Sautéed Kale

Serves 4

Fried Polenta

> ⅛ cup butter (½ stick)
> ¼ cup onion, finely chopped
> 1 garlic clove, finely minced
> 2 cups chicken stock
> 1 cup yellow cornmeal
> Salt and pepper
> Extra butter and olive oil for frying

Melt the butter in a medium-sized, heavy-bottomed pot over medium heat. Add the onion and garlic, and sauté for 3 to 5 minutes or until tender. Add the chicken broth, and bring to a boil, and gradually stir in the cornmeal. Reduce the heat to low, and cook, stirring often, for 10 minutes. Season with salt and pepper to taste. Remove from heat, and pour the mixture into a lightly greased 8" x 8" (2 quart) baking dish. Cover and chill for 2 hours or until firm. Using a 3" cookie cutter (round or square), cut out 4 pieces of the cold polenta.

Melt 1 tablespoon of butter with 1 tablespoon of olive oil in a large nonstick skillet over medium-high heat. Add the polenta pieces and cook for 2 to 3 minutes on each side or until golden brown. Transfer to a serving dish, and keep warm.

Sautéed Baby Kale

> 1 1½ lb. bag baby kale
> 2 strips thick bacon, diced
> ½ teaspoon garlic, finely chopped
> ⅛ teaspoon red pepper flakes
> ½ teaspoon red wine vinegar

In a large saucepan, bring 1 inch of water to a boil. Add the kale and cook for 3 minutes or until tender. Meanwhile, cook bacon over medium heat until crisp in a large nonstick skillet. Using a slotted spoon, remove and drain on paper towels. In the bacon drippings, sauté the garlic and red pepper flakes until fragrant and golden brown (do not let it burn).

Drain the kale and stir into the garlic mixture. Season with salt and pepper to taste. Add the vinegar and reduce to almost dry. Add the crispy bacon and stir to combine.

CHOCOLATE, COFFEE, AND CHIPOTLE BRAISED BEEF SHORT RIBS

1 lb. beef short ribs, boneless, cut into 4 4 oz. pieces
1 teaspoon cocoa powder
1 teaspoon instant espresso granules
1 teaspoon flour
½ teaspoon chili powder
½ teaspoon kosher salt
½ teaspoon black pepper
2 tablespoons olive oil
1 carrot, peeled and diced
1 celery rib, chopped
1 small onion, chopped
1 sachet with 3 sprigs of thyme, 1 bay leaf, ½ teaspoon whole peppercorn
½ small can of smoked chipotle paste
2 cups red wine
2 cups chicken stock
1 oz. bitter chocolate

In a bowl, mix together the cocoa powder, coffee granules, flour, chili powder, ½ teaspoon salt, and ½ teaspoon pepper. Dredge the pieces of meat in this mixture to coat all sides.

Heat the olive oil in a heavy-bottomed skillet and sear the pieces of meat on all sides until nice and brown. Remove the meat from the skillet and place in a baking dish large enough to accommodate the 4 pieces of meat.

In the same pan, still hot, add the vegetables and roast, stirring frequently until they are nice and caramelized. Add the roasted vegetables to the meat. Add the herb sachet. Sprinkle the leftover flour/cocoa/coffee mixture all over the meat and vegetables.

Mix the red wine and chicken stock and add the chipotle paste and stir to combine, then add the liquid mixture to the baking dish to just cover the meat.

Cover the baking dish with aluminum foil and place in a preheated 300° F oven, and braise the meat for 2½ hours or until tender.

Remove the meat and keep on a warm plate covered with foil.

Strain the braising liquid through a fine sieve into a saucepan. Skim the fat off of the surface of the sauce and reduce the sauce by three-quarters until you end up with a nice and thick sauce. Add 1oz. of bitter chocolate and stir to melt it into the sauce.

Assembly:

Divide the polenta pieces among 4 large dinner plates. Top the polenta pieces with some sautéed kale and place a piece of short rib on top of the kale. Spoon the hot sauce over the short ribs and serve. This dish can be accompanied by some buttered or roasted seasonal vegetables.

CHOCOLATE LAVA CAKE WITH RASPBERRIES, HOT CHOCOLATE SAUCE AND WHIPPED CREAM

Serves 4

> *5½ oz. butter, melted*
> *1½ cups sugar*
> *3 eggs*
> *½ teaspoon vanilla extract*
> *1½ oz. cocoa powder*
> *6½ oz. all-purpose flour*
> *1½ teaspoons baking powder*
> *⅛ teaspoon salt*
> *12 fresh raspberries, cut in half*
> *Raspberry Coulis (recipe follows)*
> *4 Chocolate Disks (recipe follows)*
> *Hot Chocolate Sauce (recipe follows)*

Whipped cream

Line a 2-quart baking dish with parchment paper.

Mix the sugar and the melted butter until combined, then whisk in the eggs, one at a time. Add the vanilla extract.

Mix the cocoa powder, flour, baking powder and salt together in a separate bowl, and then add to the butter/sugar/egg mixture, and mix until just combined (do not overmix).

Pour the batter into the baking dish and bake at 350° F in a preheated oven for about 20 to 30 minutes or until a toothpick inserted into the center comes out clean.

Remove from the oven and let cool completely.

When the cake is cool, using a round cookie cutter the size of your choice, cut out four rounds of the cake and place them on a parchment-lined tray. Using a much smaller round cookie cutter, cut a hole in the middle of each cake round.

CHOCOLATE DISKS

½ cup semisweet chocolate, chopped

Put the chocolate in a glass container and place in the microwave and turn it on for 30 seconds. At this point your chocolate is still hard. Remove the container from the microwave and stir with a fork. Put the container back into the microwave and turn it on for another 30 seconds. Your chocolate is now softer, so repeat the stirring-with-the-fork process, and put the container back into the microwave and turn it on for 10 seconds this time. Remove the container and stir the chocolate with a fork until it is completely melted.

Place a clean sheet of aluminum foil on a tray (shiny side up) and, using an offset pastry spatula, spread the melted chocolate in a uniformly thin layer and let it harden. When the chocolate is firm to the touch but not completely hard, use a round cookie cutter that is a little bit bigger than the cake round you previously cut, and cut through the chocolate, making disk marks. Place another clean sheet of foil on top of the chocolate and weight it down with a large book or other flat, heavy object. Let it dry completely until it is hard. Remove the chocolate disks and reserve.

HOT CHOCOLATE SAUCE

> *7 oz. dark bitter chocolate, chopped*
> *¾ cup whole milk*
> *1 tablespoon heavy cream*
> *1 oz. sugar*
> *1 oz. butter, diced*

Place the chocolate in a heat-proof bowl and set over a double boiler of gently simmering water and allow to melt slowly, stirring occasionally until very smooth. Take off the heat.

Combine the milk, cream and sugar in a saucepan, stir with a whisk and bring to a boil.

Pour the boiling milk mixture onto the melted chocolate, then return the mixture to the pan and let it bubble over the heat for a few seconds, stirring continuously. Turn off the heat and stir in the butter, a little at a time, until smooth and shiny. Pass it through a fine sieve and serve at once, or keep it warm in a bain-marie.

RASPBERRY COULIS

> *8 oz. fresh raspberries*
>
> *½ cup sugar*
>
> *1 tablespoon lemon juice*

Place the raspberries, the sugar, and the lemon juice in a saucepan. Turn the heat to medium and let the mixture simmer for about 10 minutes until the sugar is dissolved.

Taste the coulis, and add additional sugar if needed. Cook it until it dissolves.

Strain the coulis into a clean bowl, pushing the pulp and seeds around to drain the sauce as much as you can. Refrigerate the coulis.

Assembly:

Separate 4 large white plates, and place 1 round of chocolate cake in the center of each plate. Fill the holes in the cake with the fresh raspberries (six halves in each) and pour over some raspberry coulis. Place the chocolate disks (shiny side up) on top of the cakes. Make quenelles of whipped cream and place them nicely next to the cakes. Swirl some raspberry coulis around the cakes to make a nice presentation. Heat up the chocolate sauce until hot but not boiling, and pour into small individual creamer dishes and place them on the plates next to the cakes. Bring the dessert to the table and serve to your guests. Each person should pour their own hot chocolate sauce over the top of the cake and see the hot chocolate melt a hole in the center of the chocolate disk and run into the cake cavity mixing with the fresh raspberries.

MAESTRO MARTINO:
A TICINESE ENDS
THE CULINARY MIDDLE AGES

The Valle di Blenio in the Canton of Ticino is a broad and sunny passage leading from the south to the Lucomagno Pass and from there further to Disentis and into the valley of the Hinter Rhein, the headstream of the Rhine River. Archaeological finds reveal that the Celts even used this Alpine crossing. Since the time of the Merovingians and the Carolingians, the Valle di Blenio has been an important route between the German north and Italy. The valley served various emperors as a passage for their troops to march through for their Italian campaigns. Between 1154 and 1184, the Hohenstaufen Emperor Friedrich I Barbarossa led six expeditions to Italy. At the time of the investiture struggle between the Pope and the Emperor, the Valle di Blenio was the territory of the Milanese canons, that is, the Pope's party. The fortress Serravalle, which offered protection to the Emperor's troops and was later destroyed by the Pope's followers, was built at that time. Still today the ruins can be seen in the landscape as witnesses from a time long past.

Martino Rossi was born in that mountain valley, in the municipality of Torre, in around 1430. He is one of the most important chefs of all time. For a long time, little was known about his life, and even what we believe we know today is not well documented, but first and foremost a result of historical detective work and the art of interpretation.

When he was young, Rossi probably worked at the Hospiz San Martino Viduale, where foreign travelers found accommodations and cooking also had to be done for them. In that way, early on he came into contact with the eating habits outside of his narrow circle in the Valle de

Blenio. Via the Court of the Sforzas in Milan, Rossi's path later led to Rome, where after 1460 Rossi worked for Ludovico Trevisan, a powerful Italian cardinal and military leader who also headed the papal treasury as the Cardinal Camerlengo. Trevisan supported Pope Eugene IV in the reconstruction of Rome and provided military support in protecting the Papal States. Ludovico Trevisan's opulent banquets and receptions were well known.

Martino Rossi was one of Pope Paul II's private chefs from 1464 to 1471, and then he worked for Pope Sixtus IV at least until 1484. Both popes have an ambivalent posthumous fame. In paintings, Paul II looks extremely well nourished; according to one of the stories handed down, he is supposed to have died of devouring an excessive number of melons. The pope, for whom a career as a merchant was planned in his youth, spoke no Latin and was an opponent of humanism. We also have him to thank for introducing printing into the Papal States, though. His successor Sixtus IV was accused of favoritism, vanity, and a love of display. The Sistine Chapel, which reminds us of him to this day, came into being during the time when Rossi worked for him. Michelangelo's famous ceiling fresco was commissioned by Sixtus's nephew Julius II only later on, though. Julius II was the pope who created the Swiss Guard, which has served in Rome since 1506 and therefore can claim to be the world's longest military deployment abroad, so to speak.

After his time at the Vatican, Martino Rossi worked for Gian Giacomo Trivulzio, who later became the commander who led the French troops to victory in the Battle of Marignano in 1515. Approximately ten thousand Swiss mercenaries lost their lives in that battle. Marignano was the end of the old Swiss Confederation's expansion policy and plaied a key role in the path toward permanent neutrality according to the Swiss understanding of history. But that was a long time after Rossi used his culinary arts when working for Trivulzio.

Rossi must have been a brilliant chef and must also have been noticed in Rome. In 1475, the head of the Vatican Library at that time, Bartolomeo Sacchi, also called Platina, published a work in Latin, *De honesta voluptate et valetudine* (Of Honest Indulgence and Well-Being). The work was a big housebook with many pieces of advice and explanations. Entirely in keeping with the zeitgeist of the Renaissance, it was strongly influenced by medical knowledge. Platina's work contains many recipes which go back to Martino Rossi, who, as a chef, had no command of Latin. Platina was an honest scholar and not a plagiarist. He highly praises Maestro Martino as an incomparable master chef and mentions that he acquired a large part of his knowledge from him. Platina called Martino Rossi Martino da Como, whereas he appears as Martino da Milano in other sources. It is the same person. At that time, it was customary to state the nearest big city to the place of origin or a place of employment together with the name.

Platina's work was the first printed cookbook. It quickly found wide circulation and was soon translated into other languages as well. For a long time, however, hardly anything was known about Martino Rossi. Manuscripts written by him did not come to light until the twentieth century. His manuscripts are not written in Latin, but in a precursor to Italian. In the meantime, the *Libro de arte coquinaria*, the book on the art of cooking, has itself become a mile-stone in the history of gastronomy and Maestro Martino undeniably the most important chef of the fifteenth century. A comparison of recipes shows that a large portion of Platina's recipes actually does come from Rossi's writings.

What makes the recipes so unusual? They are a departure from the culinary culture of the Middle Ages and form the core of later Italian cuisine.

What first stands out about Martino's recipes is how precisely they are written. Most of the writings about dishes from that time which have been handed down to us are very vague, more like an entry on a menu than cooking instructions. That is not surprising since the art of cooking was handed down orally at that time. For most recipes, however, Martino made not only exact statements of quantity, but also comments about the preparation of dishes. Because clocks could not be found in kitchens at that time, Martino gave time indications by listing how many paternosters should be prayed until the dish was roasted, boiled or simmered. That penchant for practicality and precision has remained a Swiss characteristic to this day.

Many details from Martino's recipes reveal the change in the art of cooking and in eating habits. Unlike in medieval cuisine, the dishes are no longer supposed to be cooked for a long time, but should retain as much of their natural flavor as possible. In his recipe for Roman broccoli, the Maestro gives the instruction to lift the broccoli from the pot of water as soon as it is half cooked. That interest in seeing dishes and tasting them with the tongue and palate belongs to the Renaissance and its curiosity about nature, about science, and about materiality. That is why only one flavor clearly stands out in many dishes, as in Maestro Martino's Zanzarelli poultry soup.

A precise assessment of the recipe reveals still another important finding: Rossi brought together different regional culinary traditions, southern Italian, Venetian and Tuscan. In that sense, he is the first Italian chef in the history of gastronomy.

At the end of his life, the tracks come to an end. We do not know where he spent his last years. He probably returned home.

ZUCCHE FRITTE

Serves 4

>1 large zucchini, cut into ¼ inch slices
>1 large yellow squash, cut into ¼ inch slices
>1 small red onion, cut into ¼ inch slices
>4 oz. goat cheese, crumbled
>2 tablespoon extra-virgin olive oil
>Salt and pepper

DRESSING

>1½ teaspoon ground fennel
>1 small clove of garlic, finely chopped

½ slice of soft white bread
1/8 cup cider vinegar
1 tablespoon Dijon mustard
Pinch of saffron threads infused in 1 tablespoon
of hot water
½ cup olive oil

Toss the zucchini and yellow squash with 1 tablespoon of extra virgin olive oil and salt and pepper to taste.

Brush the red onion slices with the remaining extra virgin olive oil on both sides and sprinkle with salt and pepper to taste (keep the onion rounds whole).

Heat a griddle pan on the stovetop and grill the zucchini, yellow squash and onion on both sides, 3 minutes each side or until a nice grill mark is achieved on the vegetables.

Prepare the dressing by putting the bread slice cut into small dices in a blender along with the mustard, garlic, ground fennel, saffron liquid and vinegar. Blend until all is liquefied, then reduce the speed to low and start adding the olive oil slowly until the dressing is emulsified and season with salt and pepper to taste.

To put the salad together, find a round cookie cutter large enough to fit the slices of the vegetables. Place 1 slice of zucchini in the ring, some onions and some crumbled goat cheese and top with some dressing. Repeat the process with the yellow squash to finish with a slice of zucchini. There should be 2 slices of zucchini and 2 slices of yellow squash. Remove the ring revealing a nice and straight tower of squash. Drizzle the dressing over the top and around the plate. Serve with a small salad of your choosing.

RAVIOLI DI CARNE

Serves 4

> 1 lb. pork belly cut into 1 inch cubes
> 4 cups chicken stock
> 1 half chicken breast, bone and skin off, cut into
> 1 inch cubes
> 1 cup Parmesan cheese, grated
> ½ cup mozzarella, grated
> ½ tablespoon parsley, chopped
> ½ tablespoon mixed chopped fresh herbs (thyme, basil, oregano)
> ¼ tablespoon pepper
> 1/8 teaspoon ground cloves
> 1/8 teaspoon powdered ginger
> Salt
> Pinch of saffron infused in 1 tablespoon hot water
> Fresh pasta sheets (recipe follows)

PASTA DOUGH
> 2 cups all-purpose flour
> 2 large eggs
> 1 tablespoon extra virgin olive oil
> ½ teaspoon salt

Add flour and salt to a food processor bowl. Pulse 4 times to combine. Add the eggs and olive oil and run the machine until the dough is wet enough to form a ball when pressed together. Turn the dough on a flat surface (it might be crumbled but that's o.k.). Knead the dough until it comes together. Wrap in plastic wrap and let it rest at room temperature for 1 hour before using.

Set up a pasta machine and turn it to the largest opening. Cut the dough in four equal parts. Work with one piece of dough at a time and roll them into very thin sheets. Reserve on a floured flat surface covered with kitchen towels.

Put the pork in a pan with enough of the stock to cover. Put the lid on and cook for about 1 hour on medium/low heat until meat is tender. Add the chicken and continue simmering until both pork and chicken are very tender, about 30 minutes longer. Drain the meats and reserve the stock.

Work the meats in a food processor until finely chopped. Add the parmesan, mozzarella, parsley, herbs, cloves, ginger and continue mixing in the food processor until smooth. Season to taste with salt and pepper. Add a little stock if the mixture is too dry.

Lay one pasta sheet on a lightly floured flat surface and determine where the halfway point is lengthwise. Brush with egg wash to lightly wet one half of the dough. Spoon 2 teaspoons of the filling onto half of the wet side of the dough, leaving about a ½ inch between the mounds. Fold the dry half of the sheet over lengthwise to cover the filling. Press the pasta sheets together to seal the edges.

INVOLTINI

Serves 4

> *8 thin slices of veal escallops*
> *½ teaspoon ground fennel*
> *Salt and pepper*
> *3 oz. butter, softened*
> *2 tablespoons parsley, finely chopped*
> *1 teaspoon marjoram, finely chopped*
> *¼ teaspoon ground allspice*
> *Pinch of ground cloves*
> *Pinch of ground nutmeg*
> *Cooking wine*

Put the veal escallops between two sheets of parchment paper and pound them with a mallet until very thin. Sprinkle with ground fennel and salt and pepper to taste.

Cream the butter and add the parsley, marjoram, allspice, ground cloves and ground nutmeg, season with salt and pepper.

Spread the butter mixture over the veal escallops and bring the edges of the escallops to the center then roll into neat bundles and tie them with cooking twine.

To cook the rolls, add 1 tablespoon of butter into a sauté pan and heat on medium until butter is foamy. Add the rolls and cook them 4 minutes on each side, basting them with their juices all the way. Untie the twine before serving and use the juices left on the pan as the sauce.

PAN ROSTITO AL SAPOR DI FRAGOLE

Serves 4

STRAWBERRY COULIS
>2 cups strawberries, sliced
>¾ cup sugar
>1 tablespoon fresh lemon juice

FRENCH TOAST

>4 oz. cream cheese, softened
>½ cup strawberries, diced
>4 ½ inch brioche slices, from a loaf
>4 large eggs
>¼ cup sugar
>½ cup whole milk
>1 vanilla bean, split and seeded
>2 tablespoon butter

GARNISH

> *½ cup mixed berries*
> *4 mint sprigs*
> *¼ cup powdered sugar*
> *4 scoops of strawberry ice cream*

Method for the strawberry coulis:

Combine all ingredients into a saucepan and place over low heat for 15 minutes. Stir occasionally. Take from heat and cool completely. Strain the coulis through a sieve and using a rubber spatula press the strawberries through leaving only big pieces of strawberries and the seeds. Whisk the sauce to combine and refrigerate.

Method for the French toast:

Combine cream cheese and strawberries with a spoon until blended. Smear cream cheese mixture onto one side of two slices of brioche and top with the remaining slices creating 2 sandwiches. In a wide bowl, whisk together eggs, sugar, milk and vanilla seeds and set aside.

Preheat oven to 350° F.

Soak the sandwiches in the egg mixture for no longer than 20 seconds per side (brioche will fall apart if left too long in the liquid). Brown French toast on both sides in a nonstick pan with 1 tablespoon of butter for each sandwich then bake in oven for five minutes.

Use a serrated knife to cut each French toast in half. Arrange 1 toast piece on 4 dessert plates and sprinkle with powdered sugar. Serve with strawberry ice cream and fresh berries and garnish with fresh mint.

Anna Weckerin
and her
Delightful New Cookbook

The first cookbook written by a woman comes from Anna Wecker of Basel, or Weckerin in the female form customary at that time. *Ein Köstlich New Kochbuch* (A Delightful New Cookbook) of 1598 is a protestant work through and through and also suits Basel well for that reason. Anna Wecker's recipes are not intended for enjoyment, but for healthy nutrition. Apart from the beautiful woodcut frontispiece with the frequently described kitchen, there are no pictures in the book and even the decorations are far less lavish than in many other Renaissance products of the press. All those characteristics of the cookbook are not surprising when we consider the little we know about Anna Wecker.

Anna Wecker was born in Basel between 1530 and 1540 as a daughter of Isaak Keller, that is, in the years after the Reformation, which had shaped the city on the Rhine from 1529 following pressure from the guilds. Anna's exact date of birth has not been handed down. She married Johann Jakob Wecker, a doctor and scholar. In 1557, Johann Jakob Wecker became a professor in Basel and had a doctor's practice at the same time. The plague struck Basel in 1563 and 1564 and thousands of people died. In 1566, Johann Jakob Wecker took a job as City Doctor in Colmar in the Alsace. He continued to conduct scientific studies there and published medical works. The most well-known work is *Antidotarium generale & speciale* of 1585, an alchemic work which was still read and reissued even decades later. Anna Wecker followed her husband and gave him support. She accompanied him when he paid visits to patients and she helped to treat the sick. In doing so, she used her knowledge about the effect of foods. She assigned curative and protective effects to individual dishes. Rice cake, for example, was supposed to have an effect on high fever, fainting, pleuropneumonia, bad coughs and stitches in one's side. Anna Wecker was an early advocate of dietetics, the science of eating the right foods to prevent and cure diseases, an approach we will encounter again centuries later on with Bircher-Benner and his famous Birchermüesli.

Her husband encouraged her to write down her valuable knowledge and promised to support her in recording it. Anna Wecker hesitated since she did not have the appropriate training and was afraid of criticism from scientists, and because of her lack of education and linguistic proficiency. Johann Jakob Wecker died before the work was done and, with his death, the support for the project died as well. But even later on, there was no shortage of encouragement to write the work.

After her husband's death, Anna moved to the region of Nuremberg to live with her daughter, Katharina. Katharina was married to the well-known scholar Nicolaus Taurellus. It is very likely that Anna Wecker continued her work on the cookbook there and also completed it to a great extent. She died in 1596. Her cookbook was published a year later. As was usual for that time, it had a long title which generously explains the contents: *A Delightful New Cookbook: Of All Manner of Dishes /of Vegetables / Fruit / Meat / Poultry / Wild Animals / Fish and Baked Goods. To Prepare and Use Artistically and Practically Not for the Healthy Alone: But Also and in Particular for the Sick / Suffering from Illnesses and Diseases of All Kinds: Also for Pregnant Women / Those Who Have Recently Given Birth / and the Old and Weak. The Like of Which Erstwhile Never Published. Diligently Described by Mistress Anna Weckerin. Widow of Doctor Johann Jacob Wecker / of the Blessed Famous Doctor / Bereaved Widow.* The cookbook was printed in Nuremberg and soon became one of the most famous cookbooks of that era. It was reprinted several times until the late seventeenth century, sometimes supplemented with additional recipes.

What culinary art did Anna Wecker diligently describe? Her recipes are in the tradition of the northern cuisine still strongly marked by the Middle Ages. The word *vegetables* in the title does not mean vegetables in the modern sense, but "that made into mush," that is, porridges and gruels. They have little in common with the beautifully prepared and presented vegetable dishes of the Italian and French Renaissance. Almost half of the book deals with vegetables, almonds and barley, the most widespread grain at that time. Almost eighty additional recipes concern fruit, partly also exotic plants for those times such as sour oranges. Poultry and wild game, but also innards, are the predominant meat dishes, while beef, pork and mutton recipes are missing. Anna Wecker's recipes frequently require extensive cooking and chopping, as was more customary for the Middle Ages than for the Renaissance. Fish take up a small place in Anna Wecker's cookbook. In the introduction, she also stated that fish were of no great use to the sick.

Nevertheless a cookbook by a woman from Basel cannot be without salmon recipes. During Anna Wecker's lifetime, the Upper Rhine was teeming with salmon which migrated upriver to the spawning grounds. That has completely changed in the meantime. As a result of the rectification of the Rhine and damming, the previous abundance of fish has disappeared. Today it would no longer occur to any domestic worker to insist in his employment contract that salmon be served to him not more than twice a week.

Although Anna Wecker is the first female cookbook author at all and consequently ventured into a male-dominated field, she can hardly be found in feminist literature. Perhaps that is because she felt at home at the hearth and from today's standpoint played a traditional role which she also acknowledged. Her thoughts are expressed in a poem she wrote in 1586 to admonish a bride and groom, namely, the "honorable and solid young nobleman Jacob Pömern and his honorable and virtuous bride, Maid Barbara Loffelhölzin." The bride and groom not only receive useful and practical advice, for example, that a wife should not strike her husband, but also a brief discourse on gender roles. As in many wedding poems of that time, Anna Wecker begins with a Christian interpretation of the lives of Adam and Eve from Genesis. Husband and wife are not one soul in two bodies, but two souls in one body. Anna Wecker reminds the groom that his wife is a rib of his own body and a gift from God and therefore he should treat her with respect, protect her and support her. Perhaps thoughts such as those make her unattractive to feminist historiography 500 years later. But that does not alter anything about the quality of her recipes and her impact at that time, even if the language of the Renaissance sounds strange to us.

ALMOND AND SEVILLE ORANGE SOUP

Serves 4

½ cup blanched almonds, toasted
2 cups milk
1 tablespoon butter
1 large size carrot, peeled and chopped
1 celery stalk, chopped
1 small onion, chopped
¼ cup white wine
2 cups chicken stock
1 tablespoon dried Seville orange peel
½ cup fresh orange juice
2 tablespoon sherry
¼ cup cream
Salt
White pepper

Add the toasted almonds and milk to saucepan and heat up until the milk comes to a boil (do not let it boil over). Leave the pan aside for 30 minutes then add the almond milk mixture to a blender and blend until smooth and reserve.

Add the butter to a clean saucepan and then the carrots, celery and onion and cook on medium heat for 3 minutes then add the white wine and cook for 1 minute.

Add the chicken stock, the reserved almond milk and the dried Seville orange peel and cook until the vegetables are soft.

Transfer the soup to a blender and blend until smooth.

Pass the soup through a fine sieve back into the pan and cook for about 10 minutes on medium heat until the soup has thickened then and the fresh orange juice the sherry and cream.

Season the soup with salt and white pepper to taste and serve hot.

ROASTED SALMON

Serves 4

FOR THE SALMON

>*4 Salmon fillets*
>*½ cup white vinegar*
>*½ cup water*
>*1/8 teaspoon ground clove*
>*¼ teaspoon freshly ground nutmeg*
>*¼ teaspoon black pepper*
>*1 teaspoon salt*

FOR THE BROTH

>*4 cups of fish or seafood stock or broth*
>*½ cup white wine*
>*¼ cup white wine vinegar*
>*1 sprig of sage*
>*2 sprigs of flat leaf parsley*
>*Salt and pepper (to taste)*
>*1 cup heavy cream*
>*1 tablespoon unsalted butter*

Mix the vinegar and water together and wash the salmon fillets with it. Place the salmon on a tray and let it rest, covered with plastic wrap, for 30 minutes, then pat the fillets dry with paper towel and transfer to a baking dish.

Mix the clove, nutmeg, pepper and salt together and sprinkle all over the salmon fillets on both sides and let fillets dry on the baking dish, uncovered, for about 30 minutes.

Meanwhile prepare the broth by adding all ingredients, but cream, butter and one sprig of parsley, to a saucepan. Bring the liquid to a boil then reduce the heat to medium and let it simmer until the broth has reduced by 1/3. Strain the broth through a fine sieve and pour over the salmon.

Bake the salmon in a preheated 350° oven for 10 to 15 minutes until the fish is just cooked.

Remove the salmon from the baking dish and place on a plate and cover with aluminum foil.

Strain the broth into a saucepan and reduce on medium high heat by ¼. Add the heavy cream and cook until the sauce has thickened. Add the butter and emulsify it into the sauce.

Serve the Salmon with the sauce poured over the top. Chop the remaining parsley and sprinkle over the sauce.

ÄPFELKRAPFEN MIT VANILLE APFELMUS
Apple Beignets with Vanilla Apple Purée

Serves 4

3 large apples (Granny Smith or Honeycrisp preferably)
2¼ oz. flour
1/8 teaspoon salt
¼ cup carbonated water

1 egg yolk
½ teaspoon vegetable oil
1 egg white
½ cup + 3 tablespoon granulated sugar
Juice of a ½ lemon
1 tablespoon ground cinnamon
3 cups oil for frying
1 cup heavy cream
1 vanilla bean

Peel the apples and remove the core with an Apple corer (do not cut the apples in half, keep them whole)

Cut 2 of the Apples into 1/3 of an inch slices horizontally and collect 8 slices, equal in size, from the center of the apple (do not discard the smaller slices)

In a bowl, toss the 8 slices of apple with 1 tablespoon of sugar and juice of ½ a lemon and set aside.

BATTER

Add to a medium side bowl: flour, salt, carbonated water, egg yolk and vegetable oil, and whisk to combine until there are no lumps (batter should be smooth and clear of lumps. Strain the batter through a sieve if needed)

Beat the egg white until firm peaks form, and fold it into the batter very gently. Let the batter rest in the refrigerator for 30 minutes.

Strain the marinated apple slices through a sieve and pat them dry with paper towels.

Heat the Frying oil to 350 ° F.

Deep the Apple slices, one at a time, into the batter and coat them well on both sides and immerse them into the hot oil. Fry two slices at a time until nice and brown. Remove from the oil and drain on paper towels. Proceed with the remaining apple slices until they're all fried.

Mix ½ cup of granulated sugar with 1 tablespoon of ground cinnamon and dredge the fried apples in this mixture until well coated.

APPLE PURÉE

Roughly cut the last apple into chunks and combine with the remaining slices of apple that were left from the first batch (cut them into chunks as well)

Add the Apples to a saucepan with 2 tablespoons of sugar and the heavy cream. Split the vanilla bean in half and scrape the seeds out and add both seeds and bean shell to the saucepan. Cook on medium low heat until apples are soft. Keep an eye on the pan to prevent the cream from boiling over.

When apples are soft, remove the pan from the heat and let it cool completely. Use a slotted spoon to remove the apples from the pan and put them into a blender without the liquid. Start blending the apples slowly and increase the speed gradually. Add some of the cream from the pan if the purée is too thick. You want to end up with a soft and smooth purée.

Serve the Apple Beignets with Apple Purée.

VATEL AND THE SUN KING'S DELIGHTS OF THE TABLE

Vatel's life and death will always remain mysterious. The more we deal with him, the more baffling he becomes and the more definitely he escapes our judgment. To this day Vatel is well known for two magnificent, historically documented banquets for Louis XIV and for his tragic death.

Vatel's real name was Fritz-Karl Watel; his family probably originally came from the area of Zurich. The more elegant spelling François Vatel comes from the pen of Madame de Sévigné (1626-1696), whose letters are among the classics of French literature. It is also through those letters that posterity learned about Vatel's dramatic end. After the fish delivery for the great banquet for Louis XIV did not arrive on time, Vatel threw himself on his sword. To the Marquise de Sévigné, Vatel's death was a didactic drama about integrity and responsibility which should have served as an example to others. In Vatel's act of despair, an exaggerated form of a sense of duty, a particular Swiss virtue, can also be seen. Such a drama virtually calls for artistic treatment. In fact, Vatel's fate was brought to the stage many times. The film Vatel starring Gérard Depardieu and Uma Thurman came out in 2000; the film score was written by Ennio Morricone.

What do we know about the Vatel after whom hotels, restaurants, brasseries and cooking schools are named today? Vatel was probably born in Paris in 1631. At the age of 15, he learned the confectionary and catering trade. After that, he stayed in the trade for seven years. In 1653, Vatel was hired as a steward by Nicolas Fouquet. Fouquet was the French finance minister at the time when Cardinal Mazarin conducted business for the still underage Louis XIV. Fouquet spent enormous amounts of money to live at his palace in Vaux-le-Vicomte, where he also accumulated valuable paintings, jewels, rare manuscripts and antiques. Artists and writers contributed to the splendor of his court, which was frequented by Molière and La Fontaine, Madame de Scudéry and the above-mentioned Madame de Sévigné. When Cardinal Mazarin died in 1661, Fouquet expected to become the new head of government. However, Louis XIV mistrusted him, his lavish personal productions and hardly masked power ambitions. On August 17, 1661, Louis XIV was entertained by Fouquet in Vaux with an especially magnificent celebration. The formal dinner included eighty tables, 30 buffets and five courses with sumptuous dishes. The guests of honor are supposed to have eaten from solid gold tableware, the rest of the guests from silver tableware. Twenty-four violins played music by Lully. Molière's comic ballet *Les fâcheux* (The Bores) was written and given its first performance for the occasion. Vanilla-flavored sugared whipped cream, which was later known as Crème Chantilly and is regarded as Vatel's recipe, is supposed to have been served for dessert. As far as the Sun King was concerned, Fouquet's splendid self-portrayal was the straw that broke the camel's back. Three weeks later, Fouquet was arrested by Charles d'Artagnan, who inspired *The Three Musketeers* by Alexandre Dumas. An unfair trial sentenced Fouquet to banishment. Louis XIV commuted the sentence to imprisonment for life so that he could keep Fouquet under control. From 1665 to 1680, Fouquet remained in confinement in a fortress, where the mysterious man with the iron mask was available to him as a servant at times. Fouquet's household was broken up, his property confiscated.

We do not know for certain what Vatel did in the years after that. He did not reappear until 1667, this time in the service of Louis II de Bourbon-Condé (1621-1686). The Grand Condé was one of the most important military commanders of the seventeenth century and once a key figure in the Fronde, the rebellion of the nobility against Cardinal Mazarin. After the collapse of the Fronde, he was forced to flee to Spain. After Louis XIV pardoned him, he returned to France. The purpose of the banquet of 1671 was to pay homage to the king and to put an end to the past. No expenditure was too great for the fate of the House of Condé depended on the king's favor. Vatel not only saw to the kitchen, but also looked after the productions and performances. The entire court of Louis XIV with three thousand guests was invited. In the meantime, the three-day celebration has been re-searched right down to the last provable details. That is why we know about the problems in the preparation and also smaller shortcomings that occurred. Even at the beginning of the festivities, Vatel was certainly completely overtired, exhausted and thin-skinned. Fish was planned for the formal dinner on Friday, April 24, 1671, because no meat could be served due to the rules on abstaining from meat for religious reasons. Vatel did not make it easy for himself. He did not want to serve any freshwater fish such as regional salmon or trout, but wanted to impress the invited guests with saltwater fish. To do so, he sent orders to different ports and fish markets the day before. The fish were supposed to arrive at 4 a.m. the next day. However, only two baskets of saltwater fish came. Hours later, the fish were still missing. If we are to believe Madame de Sévigné's letters, after that he stepped into his room and threw himself on his sword three times to save his honor. As in a perfect drama, the fish delivery is supposed to have arrived at that moment after all. When Louis XIV finally arrived, the Grand Condé is supposed to have had tears in his eyes. Out of respect for Vatel, the fish were not eaten. To this day, we do not know where Vatel was buried.

Courtly society at the time of Louis XIV would have been less moved by Vatel's dramatic suicide if Vatel had been the simple chef he was later portrayed to be. But Vatel was more than a chef de cuisine. He was an organizer of big banquets, a sort of director of festive culinary delights, and an event manager of the Baroque age. Madame de Sévigné and the readers of her letters were undoubtedly aware of that.

Vatel is an emblematic figure in the change in the culinary arts which took place in Europe in the seventeenth century. Earlier nobility had mounted productions with expensive dishes and precious spices and had outdone one another. That fundamentally changed in the age of Baroque absolutism. The preparation of dishes became more lavish, the dishes themselves more complex. French service became generally accepted, that is, serving dishes in three courses distributed in or on many pans, bowls, boards and plates which were lavishly presented on the table. Nonculinary aspects of the dining culture of the age of Louis XIV attained great importance. The tableware, the cutlery, the tablecloths, the napkins, the centerpieces, but also the furnishings, the clothing of the noble guests, and the decor be-came central elements of the sophisticated dinner table. Music, theatrical performances and constructed sets were a part of the experience. In other words: the practices of the table were a mise-en-scène of absolutism and Baroque joie de vivre. The king was the center of the political and culinary order; table manners had strict rules and time guide-lines. Staged dinners demanded extremely complex organization, in the kitchen and when they were served. Vatel achieved all of that like very few others. Not only virtually bitter conscientiousness is a Swiss characteristic, but a talent for organization, which we also find in Oscar of the Waldorf, César Ritz, the Delmonicos and, in various forms, in the industrial food producers.

CONSOMMÉ TRANSPARENT

The Consommé Transparent was Louis XIV's favorite soup.

Serves 4

6 cups veal stock
1 oz. blanched almonds, finely chopped
½ blade of mace or a pinch of nutmeg
¼ cup vermicelli pasta
Salt
White pepper
1 tablespoon good Sherry

In a pot, bring the veal stock, mace and chopped almonds to a boil, then reduce the heat to low and let it simmer very gently for 1 hour or until the stock has deduced to half (do not let it boil or you will end up with a cloudy stock instead of a clear one).

Pass the soup through a cheese cloth and make sure you get a very clear soup. If needed pass it again through another layer of cheese cloth. Return the clear stock to the stove and bring it to a boil, reduce the heat to low and add the vermicelli. Let it simmer for about 10 minutes or until the pasta is cooked. Season with salt and white pepper and add the Sherry. Divide the consommé into 4 warm soup bowls and serve immediately.

OMELETTE AUX ASPERGES
Asparagus Omelette

Louis XIV liked asparagus enormously. In his garden (potager du roi) at the palace of Versailles many plots were permanently occupied by hot-beds for asparagus growing.

Serves 6

> *1 lb. fresh green asparagus*
> *1 small onion, diced*
> *12 eggs*
> *200 ml heavy cream*
> *2 oz. butter, divided*
> *1 bunch fresh chives, chopped*
> *2 sprigs thyme, chopped*
> *2 tablespoons flat leaf parsley, chopped*
> *Pinch of ground nutmeg*
> *Salt and pepper to taste*

Wash the asparagus and cut them into ¾ inch pieces. In a large sauté pan, on medium heat, add 1oz of butter and quickly sauté the asparagus.

Add to the sautéed asparagus the onions, half of the parsley, the chives, the thyme, the nutmeg and salt and pepper and cook over medium heat for 15 minutes stirring frequently.

Meanwhile, beat the eggs and cream together with the other half of the parsley.

Add the sautéed asparagus to the egg mixture and season with salt and pepper to taste.

In the same pan where the asparagus were cooked, melt 1oz of butter and pour in the egg and asparagus mixture. Cook over low heat until the eggs are just cooked, it should be soft but not runny, about 20 minutes.

Serve the omelet hot or cold with a green salad dressed with a lemon and orange vinaigrette.

CÔTELETTES À LA MAINTENON

Françoise d'Aubigné, Marquise de Maintenon (1635-1719) was the second wife of King Louis XIV. Her marriage to the king was never officially announced or admitted. Madame de Maintenon was very influential at court and interested in culinary art. She liked this preparation of lamb côtelettes.

Serves 4

> *8 rib lamb chops (cut from a rack of lamb)*
> *1 small onion, finely chopped*
> *¼ cup butter*
> *4 oz. button mushrooms, finely diced*
> *Salt and pepper*
> *1 cup Béchamel sauce (recipe follows)*
> *¼ cup fresh bread crumbs*

BÉCHAMEL SAUCE

> 2 ½ tablespoons butter
> 3 tablespoons flour
> 2 cups milk
> 1 teaspoon salt
> ¼ teaspoon ground nutmeg

Melt the butter in a saucepan on medium-low heat. Add the flour and stir until smooth and cook for about 4 minutes making sure the flour doesn't burn.

Meanwhile, in a separate pan, heat the milk just about to boil. Add the milk to the butter mixture ½ cups at a time, whisking continuously until very smooth and bring to a boil. Lower the heat to low and cook for 8 minutes stirring constantly. Remove from heat and season with salt and nutmeg.

Season the lamb chops with salt and pepper on both sides. Sear the lamb chops on 1 side only until brown. Place the lamb chops on a cooking sheet lined with parchment paper, uncooked side up and set aside.

Cook the onions in 1 tablespoon of butter until soft. Add 1 more tablespoon of butter to the pan and add the diced mushrooms and cook for 5 to 6 minutes. Season with salt and pepper.

Add the cooked onions and mushrooms to the Béchamel sauce and mix to combine. Spoon this mixture in equal parts on top of the uncooked side of the lamb chops and top with the bread crumbs and dot with remaining butter.

Place in a preheated 400° F oven for 8 minutes then put under the broiler until brown and bubbly. Let the meat rest out of the oven for 5 minutes, covered with aluminum foil before serving.

Serve with mashed potatoes or risotto and your favorite vegetable dish on the side.

SOUFFLÉ AUX MORILLES
Morel Soufflé

Serves 6

> *6 tablespoons butter, divided (plus extra for the soufflé dish)*
> *8 oz. morel mushrooms, finely chopped*
> *1 tablespoon shallot, finely chopped*
> *4 tablespoons flour*
> *1 cup milk*
> *1/4 tablespoon fresh thyme, chopped*
> *1 teaspoon salt*
> *1/4 teaspoon white pepper*
> *4 eggs yolks*
> *6 egg white*
> *Pinch of salt (for the egg whites)*

Preheat oven to 325° F.

Soak the Morels in salted water for 30 minutes then rinse them well and dry with paper towels.

Prepare Soufflé dish by rubbing it lightly with butter.

Sauté the mushrooms and shallots in 4 tablespoons of butter then remove it from pan and set aside.

Add the remaining 2 tablespoons of butter to the pan and add the flour. Whisk it until bubbly and lightly brown.

Add the milk and continue stirring until the mixture thickens.

Return the Shallot and morels to the pan along with the Thyme.

Remove the pan from the flame and season with Salt and White pepper.

Whisk the egg yolks until pale then whisk them into the Béchamel. Cover with plastic wrap on the surface.

Whisk all 6 of the egg whites together with a pinch of salt until firm peaks form. Fold them into the cooled Mushroom mixture.

Pour the mixture into the prepared Soufflé dish.

Place dish in a roasting pan filled half way with boiling water.

Bake for 60 minutes, or until lightly browned on top.

MERINGUES, CRÈME CHANTILLY
ET BAIES FRAÎCHES

Serves 4

> *2 large egg whites*
> *¼ tablespoon cream of tartar*
> *½ cup + 1 tablespoon of sugar*
> *2 cups mixed berries*
> *1 cup whipping cream*
> *2 tablespoons powdered sugar*
> *½ vanilla bean, seeds only (cut open and scraped)*
> *½ teaspoon vanilla extract*

Using a mixer beat the egg whites and cream of tartar, on high speed, until foamy. Gradually add ½ cup of sugar 1 tablespoon at a time, beating well after each addition. Scrape down the sides of the bowl occasionally. After adding all the sugar, continue beating until stiff shiny peaks form.

Line a baking sheet with parchment paper and mound meringue in four equal portions on the sheet leaving a space of 3 to 4 inch apart from each other. Using a clean spoon shape the mounds into 4 inch rounds and make a well in the center with the back of the spoon.

Preheat oven to 225° F.

Bake the meringues for about 1 ½ hours or until meringues are firm to the touch and sound hollow when tapped on. Turn of the oven and let the meringues cool completely inside the over. Remove from the oven when cool.

Whip the cream with 1 tablespoon of sugar, vanilla bean seeds and vanilla extract until soft peaks form.

Arrange the meringues on dessert plates and spoon some crème Chantilly inside the wells and top with the berries. Sprinkle powdered sugar over the top.

DUNAND: NAPOLEON'S CHEF AND POULET MARENGO

Was it an honor to have been Napoleon's chef? In his memoirs, Napoleon's valet Constant Wairy provides an insight into Bonaparte's eating habits. Napoleon didn't want to spend more than 8 to 10 minutes sitting at the table. He preferred eating alone and using his fingers, sopped up sauce with bread and drank wine thinned out with water along with it. No wonder that even when Napoleon was invited to dinner, he ate so quickly that the other guests had difficulty keeping in step with him.

On the military campaigns, the kitchen followed him and had to prepare meals at all times. Otherwise Napoleon didn't place any unusual demands on the kitchen; the delights of the table did not interest him very much. Fortunately Napoleon's conduct in culinary matters did not have any lasting influence on the Empire period. He refrained from forcing his own eating habits on others. On the contrary: he liked it if his important followers ran a generous household and sometimes even assumed the costs. That is why there were wonderful dinner tables in Paris again even after the decline of the *ancien régime*. Two have remained famous to this day: that of Cambacérès, the Second Consul and later Archchancellor of the Empire, and the dinners at the home of Talleyrand, the famous diplomat and foreign minister with his legendary master chef, Marie-Antoine Carême. Both of those famous dinner tables were the culinary center of attraction of the First Empire, but not an isolated case by far.

Dunand is Napoleon's well-known chef de cuisine. He, too, was a master chef who knew how to prepare wonderful meals. His father came from Switzerland and served in the French Army even during the *ancien régime*. Later he became the chef de cuisine of the Prince de Condé. That position was passed on to his son. It is the same Parisian household in which Thomas Jefferson had his chef, Hemings, trained when he was the American envoy in Paris.

The Prince de Condé was a bitter opponent of the French Revolution and one of the first noblemen who fled abroad in 1789 and operated the resistance against the Revolution and later against Napoleon's rule from there. Dunand followed the duke into exile in 1793, but obviously did not feel comfortable there and later returned to Paris. Finally he reappeared as Napoleon's chef. Two dishes call Dunand to mind to this day, even if the anecdotes surrounding the recipes are full of contradictions and inconsistencies: *Crépinettes de perdreaux* and the famous *Poulet Marengo*.

Crépinettes are flat sausages of meat filled into pork cauls. In his *Grand dictionnaire de cuisine*, Alexandre Dumas described the anecdote about the *Crépinette de perdreaux*. One day Napoleon asked Dunand why he never served pork *Crépinettes*. The baffled chef answered: because they are hard to digest and are not gastronomic. After consuming pork *Crépinettes*, it is hardly possible to work any longer. Napoleon did not want to hear of it. The next day Dunand served the desired *Crépinettes*. The pork cauls were not filled with pork, though, but with partridge.

Poulet Marengo is better known. In 1800, the Battle of Marengo, a village in the Piedmont region of northern Italy, gave Napoleon the decisive victory over the Austrians in the War of the Second Coalition. There are two legends about the origin of *Poulet Marengo*. According to one legend, because the kitchen was lost in the battle, Napoleon is supposed to have stopped off at an inn and eaten a stew of chicken, chicken broth, bread and eggs there. According to the other legend, which is more frequently quoted in the literature and was obviously also handed down by Dunand himself, Dunand is supposed to have improvised the dish immediately after the battle with the food that the dispatched soldiers could get hold of right around the battlefield. The soldiers brought back with them a young chicken, eggs, tomatoes, crayfish, olive oil, garlic and a big cooking pot. Napoleon, anyway in very good spirits after having won the battle, found the dish to be excellent. *Poulet Marengo* later became Napoleon's favorite dish that was prepared for him after every battle. Something cannot be right about this story, though. At the time of the Battle of Marengo, Dunand was not yet in Napoleon's service. After the battle, Napoleon probably actually did eat such a chicken dish and Dunand developed the well-known recipe later on. There are even assumptions that the recipe originated in the Swiss cuisine of the Jura Mountains. What is certain is that Dunand prepared the dish often. Once he left out the crayfish because he was convinced that the taste did not go well with the chicken and the sauce. Napoleon became furious, beat on the table with his fists: without crayfish the dish would bring him bad luck. The dish has long outlived Napoleon and Dunand as well. It has remained popular to this day and comes to the dinner table in many variations and developments—from simple everyday dishes to recipes developed by master chefs. The crayfish have disappeared. We have had no need to fear the emperor's dangerous outbursts of rage for a long time already. For the most part, French cuisine is divided up into *Haute Cuisine, Cuisine bourgeoise, Cuisine regionale* and *Cuisine impromptue*, that is, improvised cuisine. *Poulet Marengo* was such an improvised dish. But it has made it to the sphere of *Haute Cuisine*.

After the collapse of the empire, Dunand sought a new position. When Napoleon came back again from his exile on Elba in 1815, Dunand immediately returned to the emperor and was consequently Napoleon's chef during the Hundred Days as well. He no longer accompanied the fallen Napoleon into exile to St. Helena. Dunand felt he was too old. He returned to Switzerland. He bequeathed the table service he had received as a gift from Napoleon to the Lausanne Museum.

CONSOMMÉ MASSÉNA

André Masséna (1758-1817) was a French military commander during the Revolutionary and Napoleonic Wars once described by Napoleon as "the greatest name of my military Empire." Masséna has a special role in Swiss history. He defeated the Austrian and Russian forces in the Second Battle of Zurich (1799) after Generalissimo Suvorov failed to cross the Alps in order to reinforce the coalition. Chestnut consommé was popular at that time and recalls Masséna's military achievements during the campaigns in Italy, where chestnuts were a common food.

Serves 6

> *½ cup Madeira wine*
> *Bouquet garni (thyme, bay leaf, parsley stalks, black peppercorn)*
> *6 cups game stock*
> *3 tablespoons chestnut purée*
> *3 egg yolks*
> *¼ cup cream*
> *Salt, pepper*

Add the Madeira wine and the bouquet garni to the game stock and bring to a boil. Let it simmer for 2 hours. Season to taste.

Add the egg yolks and cream to the chestnut purée and mix to combine and season with a little salt and pepper.

Prepare six small timbale molds or ramekins and butter them well and fill them with the egg and chestnut mixture and cover with well-stretched plastic wrap, making sure it doesn't touch the egg mixture.

Place the timbales in a pan and fill the pan with hot water about ¾ of the height of the timbales. Bring the water to a simmer and poach the custard for 10 minutes or until it is set. Take them out and let them cool before unmolding.

Have six warm soup bowls ready and place one custard in each bowl and ladle some hot game broth over the custard. Serve immediately.

MOUSSELINE DE SAUMON

A mousse (French for foam) or mousseline is food prepared with whipped egg white and/or whipped cream. There are sweet dessert mousses, but also savory mousses made with fish, liver, and so forth. Mousseline became very popular in the 18th century and remained so during the great era of classical French cuisine.

Serves 4

> *3½ oz. salmon fillet (skinless, boneless and cut into cubes)*
> *1 egg white*
> *½ shallot, thinly sliced*
> *1 teaspoon thyme, finely chopped*
> *1 cup heavy cream, chilled*
> *Salt, white pepper*

Place the salmon, egg white, shallots and thyme into a food processor bowl and process to a smooth paste. With the machine running, slowly add the cream until combined. Season with salt and white pepper to taste. Pass the paste through a sieve into a bowl to obtain a clean and very smooth mousse. Cover the bowl with plastic wrap and chill in the refrigerator for about 1 hour.

Preheat the oven to 275° F.

Brush 4 ramekins with melted butter and fill each one by two-thirds with the salmon mousse and tap the ramekins firmly on a hard surface to eliminate air bubbles. Place the ramekins in a baking pan and pour boiling water to come up two-thirds of the ramekins. Cover with aluminum foil and bake until firm to the touch and it looks a little puffed up, about 14-15 minutes. At this point you can let it cool a little and serve the mousseline warm or let it chill completely in the refrigerator and serve it chilled with a salad of your choosing.

To unmold the mousseline, run a knife around the sides of the ramekins and turn it down on a serving plate.

POULET MARENGO

Serves 4

> 2 tablespoons olive oil
> 1 large onion, finely chopped
> 3 garlic cloves, finely chopped
> 1 ½ lb. whole chicken, cut up
> ¼ cup flour
> 1 teaspoon thyme, finely chopped
> 1 bay leaf
> 1 lb. fresh tomatoes, peeled, seeded and diced
> ½ lb. button mushrooms, sliced
> ½ cup white wine
> 1 cup chicken stock
> 2 tablespoons butter
> Juice of 1 lemon
> 3 teaspoons parsley, chopped
> Salt, pepper
> 4 fried eggs
> 4 heart-shaped croutons

Lightly season the chicken pieces with salt and pepper. Add the olive oil into a sauté pan and sear the chicken to a nice brown color on both sides. Remove and set aside.

In the same pan, using the fat from the chicken, add the onions and reduce the heat to medium and cook until soft without letting it burn. Add the flour and stir to combine and let it cook for about 2 minutes, stirring constantly. Add the white wine and whisk until the flour is dissolved and let it cook for 1 minute, then add the chicken stock and whisk to combine. Add the chopped thyme and bay leaf.

Place the chicken pieces in the pan and mix it into the sauce. Cover the pan and cook it for about 10 minutes on medium heat.

Add the tomatoes and mushrooms to the pan and stir to mix. Cover and let it all cook together until the chicken is cooked through and flaky when pierced with a fork.

Uncover the pan, add the lemon juice and let the sauce reduce a little until thick, then turn off the heat and add the butter and stir to emulsify into the sauce. Adjust the seasoning if needed and sprinkle with chopped parsley.

Serve the chicken pieces on plates topped with a fried egg and a heart-shaped crouton.

GLACE AU POMME TALLEYRAND-PÉRIGORD

This ice cream is named after the famous diplomat Charles Maurice de Talleyrand-Périgord (1754–1838). His career spanned the reign of Louis XVI, the years of the French Revolution, and the reigns of Napoleon, Louis XVIII, and Louis-Philippe. Napoleon distrusted Talleyrand, but found him extremely useful in the pursuit of his political ambitions. The name "Talleyrand" has become a byword for deceitful, cynical diplomacy. The ice cream *Glace au Pomme Talleyrand-Périgord* is served in many different ways, often in hollowed and candied apples.

Serves 6-10

2 lb. apples
2 oz. butter
3 oz. sugar
½ oz. Calvados
2 cups crème anglaise (recipe follows)

CRÈME ANGLAISE
  2 cups heavy cream
  1 cup half and half
  2/3 cup sugar
  1 tablespoon vanilla extract
  6 egg yolks

In a bowl, whisk egg yolks and sugar to combine.

In a heavy-bottomed saucepan, on medium heat, simmer the cream and half and half until it comes to a boil. Remove from heat and add a little bit of the hot cream to the egg yolk mixture and whisk to combine. Slowly add the remaining hot cream to the yolks, whisking constantly until all is combined.

Pour the egg and cream mixture back into the saucepan and cook it on medium heat, stirring constantly until the cream thickens and coats the back of a wooden spoon. Do not let the cream boil or it will scramble the eggs. Immediately pour the cream into a bowl and place the bowl in an ice bath to stop the cooking process. Here you have a crème anglaise which is the basis for the ice cream.

Peel the apples and cut them into quarters.

Sauté the apples with sugar and butter until caramelized, then add the calvados to deglaze.

Let the apples cool, then mash them with a fork or a potato masher.

Add the mashed apples to 2 cups of crème anglaise and mix to combine. Refrigerate the apple mixture for at least 3 hours.

Add the chilled apple mixture to an ice cream maker and proceed according to manufacturer's instructions.

DELMONICO'S AND HAUTE CUISINE
IN THE NEW WORLD

When Delmonico's Restaurant was closed because of Prohibition in 1923, a history spanning nearly a hundred years came to an end. Nothing had left more of a mark on the development of the restaurant culture and haute cuisine in the United States than Delmonico's. Still today dishes such as *Delmonico Steak*, *Delmonico Potatoes*, and *Lobster Newberg* recall the restaurant's heyday. As a result of the ban on alcohol, the guests stayed away. They preferred to dine with wine at home.

Emigrants from the Canton of Ticino founded Delmonico's and made it famous in gastronomic circles. The history of Delmonico's is also the history of the Delmonico family, a complicated family saga with many and very different figures and fates.

Giovanni Del-Monico from the small Ticinese village of Mairengo comes at the beginning of the legend. When he was young, he traveled around the world as a captain. In 1824, he settled down at the southern tip of Manhattan. He opened a wine shop, filled wine from barrels into bottles which he sold individually. After three years, he closed the shop and went back to Switzerland. But he did not stay in Switzerland for long. With his brother Pietro, who ran a confectioner's shop in Bern, he decided to go back to New York and open a new business. They both pitched in their money and crossed the Atlantic. In 1827, they opened a café with a confectioner's shop. The café did well, but the two brothers had bigger ambitions and soon opened a restaurant. At that time, the United States just had restaurants where only one set meal was served. They were the first to introduce menus from which the guests could select dishes. There had been such restaurants in France for some time, but they were a pioneering innovation for the U.S. The Delmonico brothers were obviously also the first to introduce a separate wine list in the U.S. Their system was quickly copied. But menus alone are not sufficient for culinary success. The dishes themselves are more important. Although it was already known beforehand, the Delmonicos spread French cuisine around the U.S. They attached great importance to excellent quality in ingredients and preparation. "Quality is more important than price" was their motto. They imported much food from Europe, also luxury goods such as expensive Bordeaux wines and champagne. Later on they bought a farm in Brooklyn to cultivate vegetables that were not available on the market otherwise. The dishes were served on expensive china and eaten with silver cutlery, surrounding them with a special aura.

In their history spanning nearly a hundred years, the Delmonicos ran restaurants at ten locations in all, four restaurants simultaneously at certain times. The restaurants followed the development of the settlement of New York from the southern tip of Manhattan upward.

The most important Delmonico was Lorenzo, John and Peter's nephew. He arrived in New York in 1834, when he was only nineteen years old. After that, he ran the family business for forty years, making it very famous. He was a man who had a great capacity for work, but also a meticulous passion for details. He adhered to a strict, unalterable schedule. He arrived at the market at four o'clock in the morning, supervised the buying of meat and then returned to the restaurant at eight o'clock. At 9 a.m., he went home and then in the evening he was back at the restaurant, where he looked after the guests and made sure that everything ran smoothly until midnight.

In 1849, Lorenzo Delmonico hired his Ticinese compatriot Alessandro Filippini as the new chef de cuisine. Filippini came from Airolo, at the northern end of the canton near the southern portal of the St. Gotthard Pass. In 1880, Filippini published his first cookbook, the *Delmonico Cook Book*. After having worked for nearly forty years, Filippini retired in 1888 and began to write more cookbooks, which are worth reading to this day. The most well-known cookbook is *The Table: How to Buy Food, How to Cook It, and How to Serve It*. It provides a good insight into the dishes that were prepared at Delmonico's at that time. In 1862, Lorenzo Delmonico was able to engage a perhaps even more well-known chef for his restaurant, the Alsatian Charles Ranhofer.

The 1860s and the 1870s were the heyday of Delmonico's. No other restaurant in the New World could keep up. Delmonico's had become the meeting place of the rich and famous. The Vanderbilts, the Rockefellers, the Morgans, the Astors, the Goodyears, Samuel Morse, Theodore Roosevelt, European nobility, and writers such as Charles Dickens, Oscar Wilde and Mark Twain were among the guests.

Lorenzo Delmonico died in September 1881. There is a grave which he paid for in the cemetery of his native village, Mairengo. However, he was buried in the family grave in New York and 20,000 mourners followed the coffin. Extensive obituaries appeared in the newspapers. The family business was taken over by Lorenzo's nephews.

At the turn of the century, business got worse and worse. The change at the top, the many family disputes and difficulties are well documented and were the subject of gossip and the tabloids at that time. From today's perspective, they are not particularly interesting anymore.

The outbreak of World War I brought about an additional crash. In 1919, the family business went bankrupt. What remained was sold to a proprietor of a restaurant. By chance, the transfer exactly coincided with the day when Prohibition was introduced. With that, too, the end of Delmonico's was irrevocably sealed.

Fortunately the culinary inheritance of Delmonico's is in good hands with the books by Filippini and Ranhofer. *Delmonico Steak* is the most well-known of the dishes. It is a boneless sirloin steak of approximately five centimeters in thickness with fine marbling. The right cut is what is decisive about *Delmonico Steak*. It is supposed to be the cut that was used at Delmonico's in 1840; however, there are at least a half dozen different cuts said to be the original. Even Ranhofer's masterpiece, *The Epicurean*, contains three different types of preparation for *Delmonico Steak*.

Lobster Newberg, Lobster à la Newberg or *Lobster à la Delmonico*, a dish made from lobster, butter, cream, cognac, sherry and egg, seasoned with cayenne pepper, is known to this day. The recipe is supposed to have originally come from Ben Wenberg, a captain engaged in the fruit trade. In 1876, he introduced the dish to Charles Delmonico, the hotel manager at that time. It was improved by Charles Ranhofer and finally appeared on the menu as Lobster à la Wenberg. As a result of an argument between Wenberg and Charles Delmonico, the dish had to be removed from the menu again. Since the lobster had won many enthusiasts in the meantime and the guests asked for it, it reappeared on the menu with its initial letters reversed: hereafter and to this day it has been called Lobster Newberg instead of Lobster Wenberg.

Filippini dedicated dishes to individual members of the Delmonico family: Lorenzo, Charles Constant, Aimée, Rosa, and Josephine Delmonico. No one knows them anymore today.

LOBSTER NEWBERG

Serves 4

    4 small lobster tails, uncooked
    2 tablespoons unsalted butter
    ½ medium onion, chopped
    1 stalk celery, chopped
    1 medium leek, white part, washed and diced
    2 medium carrots
    4 fresh tarragon sprigs
    1 tablespoon flour
    1/4 cup dry sherry
    1 teaspoon tomato paste
    ¼ cup heavy cream
    ½ teaspoon salt

1/8 teaspoon white pepper
1 large egg yolk

Fill a large pot ¾ full with cold water. Set over high heat and bring to a boil.

Prepare an ice bath.

Add the lobster tails to the pot, making sure that each one is completely submerged in water and cook for 3 minutes. Transfer lobsters to ice bath to cool and drain in a colander.

Carefully remove lobster meat from the tails. Cut the meat into bite-size pieces and refrigerate, covered with plastic, until ready to use. Reserve the shells from the tails for making stock.

Melt 1 tablespoon of butter in a large saucepan set over medium heat. Add chopped onions and celery to pan. Coarsely chop ½ leeks and 1 carrot and add to pan. Add reserved lobster shells, 2 sprigs tarragon, and enough water to cover shells by 3 inches. Bring liquid to a boil, reduce heat, and simmer, skimming surface often until the stock is flavorful, about 1 hour.

Prepare an ice bath. Strain stock through a fine sieve, pushing down on solids to extract liquid. Transfer stock to a clean saucepan, and discard solids. Continue cooking stock until liquid has reduced to 1 cup. Remove from heat, and transfer to ice bath to chill. Transfer chilled stock to an airtight container and refrigerate until ready to use.

Split the remaining leek lengthwise. Cut the leek and remaining carrot into ½ inch pieces and set aside.

Melt the remaining 1 tablespoon of butter in a medium saucepan set over medium-low heat. Sprinkle flour into saucepan, and cook, stirring constantly, so mixture foams and forms a paste but does not turn brown, about 2 minutes.

Carefully add sherry, stirring constantly to loosen any flour that has cooked onto the bottom of saucepan, being careful that no lumps form. Add tomato paste and 1 cup of the reserved lobster stock. Add the chopped leek and carrot to the saucepan, and cook until just tender, about 5 minutes. Stir in cream, and bring to a boil. Reduce heat, and simmer until sauce just starts to thicken, 5 to 6 minutes. Add salt and white pepper. Pick tarragon from remaining 2 sprigs, chop, and add.

In a small bowl, whisk egg yolk. Add a ladleful of hot sauce to temper the yolk and whisk to combine. Return mixture to saucepan over low heat; whisk to combine.

Remove from heat.

Preheat oven to 350 degrees. Set four 6-ounce ramekins into a large roasting pan.

Add the reserved lobster meat to the sauce; stir to combine. Divide the Newberg evenly among the ramekins. Transfer the roasting pan to oven, and pour 1 inch boiling water into the roasting pan. Cook until the Newberg bubbles, about 20 minutes. Remove roasting pan from the oven and carefully transfer ramekins to serving plates. Serve the Newberg immediately with croutons or biscuits.

ENDIVE, WATERCRESS AND APPLE SALAD

Serves 4

> *2 Belgian endive, cored and julienned*
> *1 cup watercress, tough stems removed*
> *1 Granny Smith apple, cored and julienned*
> *½ tablespoon lemon thyme leaves*
> *1½ tablespoons fresh lemon juice*
> *1½ tablespoons fresh lime juice*
> *1 tablespoon white wine vinegar*
> *1 tablespoon honey*
> *1 tablespoon Dijon mustard*
> *½ cup extra virgin olive oil*
> *Salt, pepper*

Combine and mix the lemon juice, lime juice, vinegar, honey, and mustard in a bowl. Slowly add the olive oil in a steady stream, whisking constantly until emulsified. Season with salt and pepper to taste.

In a bowl, combine the endive, watercress, apple and lemon thyme and add just enough vinaigrette to coat the salad. Test the salad for seasoning and add more if needed.

Divide the salad on 4 plates and drizzle with more vinaigrette around the edges.

DELMONICO STEAK

Serves 4

> *2 prime rib-eye steaks*
> *2 tablespoons extra virgin olive oil*
> *Sea salt*
> *Black pepper*
> *1 tablespoon butter*

MEAT BUTTER
> *1 small fresh bay leaf*
> *¼ tablespoon fresh thyme*
> *1 tablespoon sea salt*
> *¼ lb. unsalted butter, soft*

Pat the steaks dry and season with salt and pepper.

Put the olive oil in a frying pan on high heat until the oil starts to smoke and add the steaks. Sear the steak on one side for 3 minutes, then turn over and sear the other side for another 3 minutes. Turn the heat to medium and add 1 tablespoon of butter and swirl the pan around so the butter melts into the fat released from the meat. Spoon the melted butter on top of the steaks, basting them all over for another

1 to 2 minutes. Take the steaks out of the pan and let them rest covered with aluminum foil for 5 to 6 minutes.

To make the Meat Butter: Place the sea salt, bay leaf and thyme in a spice grinder and grind until all turns into a powder. Add the salt mixture to the soft butter and mix to combine. Put the butter on a piece of plastic film and roll it up to form a log. Place in the refrigerator to harden. When hard, cut slices and leave out at room temperature to soften again just before use.

Slice the steaks against the grains and divide equal portions on 4 plates. Place a slice of the soft meat butter on top of the warm meat and let it melt into the meat. Serve with your favorite starch dish and some vegetables.

BAKED ALASKA

Secretary of State Seward is well remembered for the acquisition of Alaska from Russia nicknamed "Seward's Folly" or "Seward's Icebox" at that time. To commemorate the purchase, Delmonico's chef Charles Ranhofer created "Baked Alaska," a dessert made from ice cream placed on a pie dish lined with slices of sponge cake and covered with meringue. "Baked Alaska" is one of Delmonico's best known recipes.

Serves 4

> 4 individual dessert sponge cakes
> 4 tablespoons strawberry preserves
> 4 scoops vanilla ice cream
> 3 egg whites
> ½ cup sugar
> ¼ teaspoon salt
> Blueberry sauce (recipe follows)

BLUEBERRY SAUCE

>	*1 cup fresh blueberries*
>	*¼ cup sugar*
>	*½ tablespoon fresh lemon juice*
>	*Pinch of salt*
>	*¼ teaspoon vanilla extract*

In a pan, add blueberries and sugar and crush the berries. Add lemon juice and salt and bring the mixtures to a boil. Boil for 2 minutes. Turn heat off and add vanilla and mix. Chill the sauce completely before using it.

Set cakes on a baking sheet lined with parchment paper. Place 1 tablespoon of strawberry preserves into each cake. Top the cake with a scoop of ice cream. Top each scoop of ice cream with a little blueberry sauce and take the sheet pan to the freezer.

Beat egg whites until foamy and gradually start adding the sugar, then add the salt. Continue beating until firm peaks form and meringue is shiny. Take the ice cream out of the freezer and, working quickly, cover each dessert completely with meringue, making sure you leave no gap or air spaces. Return to freezer.

Preheat oven to 425° F. Place the baking sheets with the desserts in the oven and bake for 6 to 8 minutes or until meringue is lightly browned. Serve immediately with fresh berries and blueberry sauce.

JOSEPH FAVRE: THE REVOLUTIONARY AND HIS CULINARY DICTIONARY

Joseph Favre was a man who sought progress all his life. He sought it through revolutionary political ideas, but also in his trade, culinary art. He is among the classics of culinary art and is often mentioned in the same breath with such important personalities as Carême, Dugléré, Dubois, and Escoffier. Without the ideas and experiences he got from his political activities, his culinary career would also have been different.

In the second half of the nineteenth century, Switzerland was one of the few democratic states. Located in the middle of Europe, the young federal state was a place of refuge for all kinds of politically persecuted individuals. The spectrum of those immigrants was great; it ranged from Russian anarchists and Italian independence fighters to people such as Richard Wagner and Louis Napoleon. At that time, Joseph Favre was born in the Canton of Valais in 1849 as the illegitimate child of a priest. As an orphan, a higher education was not open to him. A priest or a tradesman—that was the choice he had. Thus he did a three-year apprenticeship as a chef at a hotel in Sion, the capital of the Canton of Valais. Later on he never lost his enthusiasm for culinary art.

Favre was a lively intellectual with broad interests and great curiosity. He also kept those characteristics throughout his life. After the apprenticeship, he went to Geneva and took up a job at the well-known Hotel Metropol, which is still among the big five-star hotels of the city on the Rhône today. At the same time, he began to attend natural science lectures as an auditor at the University of Geneva. He changed his chef positions in rapid succession. He often took a job only for the summer season and returned to Geneva in the winter to continue his education at the university. In Paris, he worked at the well-known La

Milanese restaurant on the Boulevard des Italiens, then for a famous caterer. He also found positions at big hotels and restaurants in Wiesbaden and London and later in Switzerland. In that way, Joseph Favre came into contact with the world of the chic and the wealthy. But there was a second world for him. Wherever he stayed, he sought contact with revolutionary and anarchistic circles; that is why his name appears not only in the history of culinary art, but also in the history of revolutionary movements.

When he worked in Clarens in 1874, he became a member of the Vevey section of the First International. A year later, he worked at the Hotel du Parc in Lugano, where the brother of the Italian anarchist Nabruzzi also worked. In the same year, Favre was a cofounder of the magazine *L'Agitatore* and of the Lugano section of the International. A dinner that he prepared for well-known anarchists and revolutionaries took place at that time. A heterogeneous dinner for a heterogeneous group of guests, as Favre later recalled. Perhaps the two most influential anarchists at that time were guests: Mikhail Bakunin, who was in poor health and died in Bern a year later, and Errico Malatesta, whose ideas were similar to Bakunin's and whose influence spread beyond Italy to all of Europe at the end of the nineteenth century and the beginning of the twentieth century. The two French Communards Benoît Malon and Arthur Arnould as well as Jules Basile Guesde, a Marxist and one of the key figures among the French socialists, were also invited to the dinner. Élisée Reclus, who had to leave France because of his political beliefs, was an especially close friend of Favre's. Reclus was a geographer and an important scientist. Over a period of almost twenty years, he created his great 19-volume work *La nouvelle géographie universelle* and, despite his political persecution, received the much sought-after gold medal of the Geographical Society of Paris, the oldest geographical society in the world. His life and work undoubtedly inspired Favre to write a similarly monumental work about culinary art.

Back to the dinner in Ticino; the guests not only differed in their political opinions. They also had very different preferences regarding food and drink. Malon and Arnould drank red Barolo wine. Malatesta,

Guesde (and Favre) drank sparkling wine. Élisée Reclus contented himself with water and Bakunin drank a beer at first, then tea, and surrounded the group with the smoke from his Turkish cigarettes. The guests included vegetarians and meat lovers, ascetics and gourmets. Favre himself cooked. He served deep-fried fish from Lake Lugano, a risotto and a pudding. The dinner is primarily known for its dessert, *Salvator pudding*. The name of the pudding refers to the mountain Monte San Salvatore in Lugano, at the foot of which Favre cooked the dinner. Unlike all the other dishes and drinks, the pudding is supposed to have been met with general approval and even praise.

A year later, Favre worked as a chef at the Hotel Zähringen in Fribourg and prepared a meal for a completely different table. Empress Eugénie, who had lost her throne after the Franco-Prussian War, and Félix Dupanloup, Bishop of Orléans, were the guests. Favre cooked a Vol-au-vent with béchamel sauce and a duck dish with foie gras for the light meal. The bishop thought that one could not have eaten better even in heaven and concluded that the chef was not only extraordinarily capable, but also had to be religious. When the bishop then learned that Favre's piety was nothing to write home about, he said that the Vol-au-vent had been "diabolically good." That was probably the recipe that Favre also included in his work later on.

Although Favre was also a good chef, his achievement consists less in new recipes than in his systematic reappraisal of culinary knowledge and in organizing chefs with the aim of improving culinary art. For Favre, culinary art was less a trade than a science. In 1877, he began to publish the journal *La Science culinaire* in Geneva; he also launched the journal *Le Socialisme progressif* through a publishers' collective almost simultaneously. It was the very first time that a professional chef published a specialist journal. Favre encouraged his colleagues themselves to write for the journal. He proposed exhibitions and competitions among chefs. In 1879, Favre founded the *Union universelle pour le progrès de l'art culinaire*. Eighty sections were founded around the world later on. The same approach also used by revolutionary movements can be seen in Favre's working method. Progressive ideas were supposed to be helped on the road to success by activists organizing themselves internationally and by using a joint publication as a platform for discussions regarding content. The Paris section of the Union universelle pour le progrès de l'art culinaire served as a sort of headquarters for the network. Favre was secretary-general at first, but there was a dispute after a short time and he was expelled with five other members. He was accused of trying to bring about a split in the section, of giving public and free cooking classes and of having revealed chefs' professional secrets by doing so. Such episodes and power struggles were also not unknown to revolutionary movements at that time. As a counter project, Favre then founded the *Académie culinaire de France*, which is the oldest chefs' organization in the world today. It is active in twenty-seven countries and has almost a thousand members. Its aim is to perfect French cuisine.

Joseph Favre spent the last years of his life in Boulogne-sur-Seine and worked on his life's work, the *Dictionnaire universel de cuisine pratique: encyclopédie illustrée d'hygiène alimentaire*. Even if recipes make up a considerable part of the text, the book is not a cookbook in the narrow sense. The subtitle reveals what mattered to Favre: Modification de l'homme par l'alimentation, changing a person through diet, his physical and emotional improvement. The *Dictionnaire universel* contains many precise comments covering the state of food science, hygiene, but also medical knowledge at that time, in addition to many comments on cultural history. Many articles in the Dictionnaire are based on Favre's earlier published work and on articles in *La Science culinaire*. The work comprising nearly two thousand pages and more than five and a half thousand recipes is a standard work on the history of gastronomy, equally important as the works by Carême and Dubois, whom Favre admired. Favre did not live to see the publication of his work. He died shortly before it was published in 1903. The *Dictionnaire universel* has become a monument to him.

VOL AU VENT À LA BÉCHAMEL

Serves 4

> *4 puff pastry shells (store bought)*
> *1 tablespoon butter*
> *2 slices cooked ham, cut into small dices*
> *2 cups mushrooms (your choice), thinly sliced*
> *1 teaspoon thyme, finely chopped*
> *½ garlic clove, finely chopped*
> *½ shallot, finely diced*
> *2 tablespoon Cognac*
> *Salt, pepper to taste*
> *1 tablespoon parsley, finely chopped*
> *¼ cup grated Gruyère cheese*

BÉCHAMEL

> *2 cups milk*
> *1 oz. flour*
> *1 oz. butter*

Bake the puff pastry shells according to package instruction. After baked, carefully cut out the cap on the top and reserve. Remove the inside dough from the shells creating a well. Be careful not to pierce the bottom, leave the bottom layer intact.

Sauté the shallots and garlic in 1 tablespoon of butter on medium low heat until soft. Add the mushrooms and cook until ten-der and liquid has reduced to almost dry. Add the thyme and cognac and cook until the liquid has reduced completely. Add the ham and season with salt and pepper to taste. Reserve.

In a saucepan, on medium low heat, melt the butter. Add the flour and mix to combine and cook, without burning, for 2 minute. Gradually add the milk, whisking continuously, and cook the sauce until thickened.

Add the mushroom and ham mixture to the béchamel and mix to combine. Add the chopped parsley.

Place the puff pastry shells on a sheet tray lined with parchment paper and fill each shell with the béchamel sauce. Divide the Gruyère cheese among the four shells on top of the sauce, and place the reserved pastry caps on top.

Bake for 5 minutes on a preheated 350° F oven. Serve warm with a salad.

GIGOT DE MOUTON À L'ITALIENNE

Serves 4

1 cup breadcrumbs, dried
¼ cup milk
½ cup Pecorino Romano
2 cloves of garlic, finely chopped
2 cups button mushrooms, sliced
2 tablespoons Italian parsley, chopped
3 lb. boneless leg of lamb, butterflied
3 tablespoons olive oil
1 cup onion, chopped
2 bay leaves
1 tablespoons spring rosemary, finely chopped
1 tablespoons thyme, finely chopped
3 cups fresh tomatoes, peeled, seeded and diced
½ cup white wine
3 cups chicken stock
1 tablespoons white truffle oil
Salt, pepper

Sauté the mushrooms in 1 tablespoon of olive oil until soft. Add ½ tablespoon of garlic and cook for 2 minutes. Remove from heat and let cool.

Put the breadcrumbs in a bowl and pour in the milk and let it soak for a few minutes until the bread crumbs have absorbed the all milk. Squeeze the milk out of the bread-crumbs as much as you can and get rid of the left over milk in the bowl. Put the moist breadcrumbs back to the bowl and add the Pecorino Romano, cooled mushrooms and the chopped parsley and mix to combine into a paste. Season with salt and pepper to taste.

Lay out the butterflied leg of lamb and trim any thick fat from the outside surface and leave a thin layer of fat. Place the bread crumb mushroom mixture and spread to cover the whole inside of the meat leaving a margin around the edge. Roll up the meat to form a log with the filling tightly enclosed inside and secure the meat with cooking twine around the log every few inches along its length. Season the outside with salt and pepper to taste.

Pour the remaining olive oil in a pan big enough to fit the whole meat and on medium heat sear the meat on all sides until brown. Remove the meat from the pan and set it aside.

In the same pan over medium heat add the onions and cook until soft. Add the remaining garlic and cook for two minutes. Add the white wine and reduce to almost dry. Add the tomatoes, rosemary and thyme and cook for 3 minutes. Add the chicken stock and mix to combine. Add the meat to the pan and reduce the heat to medium-low and cover the pan. Simmer for 1 ½ hours, or until the meat is tender. Rotate the meat in the pan every now and then.

When meat is cooked, remove it from the pan and place it on a platter to rest covered with aluminum foil.

Meanwhile, reduce the sauce to a thick sauce consistency and add the truffle oil and whisk to emulsify.

Remove the twine from the meat and slice it crosswise into 1 inch thick slices and arrange them on a platter and pour the sauce over the top.

Serve with risotto.

SALVATOR PUDDING

Serves 4

> 1 gâteau de Compiègne (recipe follows)
> 2 tablespoon apricot marmalade
> 2 tablespoon Maraschino liqueur
> ¼ cup candied ginger, chopped
> ¼ cup candied Angelica, chopped
> 2 cup milk
> ½ cup sugar
> 2 whole eggs
> Maraschino Sabayon (recipe follows)

GÂTEAU DE COMPIÈGNE

> 5 ¼ oz. flour
> 3 ½ oz. butter, soft and cubed
> ¾ oz. sugar
> Pinch of salt
> 2 eggs
> 1 egg white
> 0.17 oz. east
> 1 ½ oz. heavy cream

Warm the cream to lukewarm and add 1 tablespoon of sugar and east and let it foam and rise, about 10 minutes.

Add the flour to a mixing bowl of an electric mixer with a paddle attached and add the rest of the sugar and salt and mix to combine.

Mix the eggs and egg white into the east and cream mixture and add half of this mixture to the flour and turn the machine on to low speed and start kneading the dough. When all is incorporated, add the remaining egg and cream mixture and increase the speed to medium and continue kneading the dough until it's elastic, smooth and shiny, about 6 minutes.

Gradually add the pieces of butter and keep running the machine just until the butter is incorporated into the dough.

Turn the dough out into a bowl, cover with plastic and let it rise on a warm place until it has doubled in volume, about 1 hour. Refrigerate the dough for 30 minutes.

Butter an 8" X 2" round cake pan and put the dough in it spreading it evenly in the pan. Cover and let it rise again until doubled.

Preheat the oven to 350° F and bake the cake for about 30 minutes until the top is brown, then turn off the oven and leave the cake inside for 15 minutes.

MARASCHINO SABAYON

>*4 egg yolks*
>*3 tablespoon sugar*
>*2 tablespoon Maraschino liqueur*
>*¼ whipping cream*

Add the egg yolks to a metal bowl and whisk in the sugar and Maraschino liqueur to combine. Place the bowl on top of a double boiler on low heat and whisk vigorously until the yolks are cooked and doubled in volume. Take the bowl off the heat every now and then to prevent the eggs to overcook and scramble. When eggs are cooked, take the bowl off the heat and set it aside. Whip the cream until soft peaks form and gently fold it into the sabayon. Refrigerate.

Salvator Pudding Method:

Cut 2 ½ inch slices of the Gateau horizontally and then with a cookie cutter that is the size of a ramekin cut 8 rounds.

Place 1 round of the gateau on the bottom of 4 ramekins.

Mix the apricot preserve with 2 tablespoons of Maraschino liqueur and spread on top of the gateau inside the ramekins.

Divide the candied ginger and Angelica amongst the 4 Ramekins.

Cut some of the leftover gateau into small dices and add to the ramekins mixing with the candied fruits.

CÉSAR RITZ: KING OF HOTELIERS AND HOTELIER TO KINGS

The name Ritz is short and catchy. To this day it is a trademark for glamour and a chic lifestyle. In English, the adjective "ritzy" means elegant, and since the early '30s Irving Berlin's jazz song *Puttin' on the Ritz* (getting dressed for the Ritz, getting dressed up) has been rerecorded countless times by show business greats from Fred Astaire, Clark Gable, Ella Fitzgerald, Judy Garland, and Benny Goodman to Robbie Williams and others.

Who was César Ritz? In old portraits, he appears to be what he was: an entrepreneur of the "Gilded Age." Like nobody else, César Ritz shaped the world of the grand hotels and has left his mark to this day. His life story was not predestined. He was born in a small village in the Canton of Valais as the thirteenth child in a shepherd's family. When he was still very young, his parents sent him to an inn in Brig, the capital of Upper Valais, where he worked as a sommelier; however, he was soon thrown out because it was explained to him that nothing would become of him in the gastronomy business.

From then on, César Ritz began to discover the world and later create his own world of hotels. He was only seventeen years old when he went to Paris for the world exhibition and found a job first as a waiter, then as a sommelier. Later he got a job at the famous Parisian hotel Le Splendide, and when he was barely twenty years old he became the maître d'hôtel at the Chez Voisin restaurant on the Rue Saint-Honoré.

At upscale restaurants at that time, the maître d'hôtel was a type of head waiter who looked after the welfare of the guests in a comprehensive way and not yet a business manager performing tasks. The maître d'hôtel supervised the quality of the services and he himself performed sensitive operations such as flambéing and carving. That was how César Ritz came into contact with the upper class. Throughout his life, knowing his guests and being able to translate their wishes into business models remained one of his strengths. In the years that followed, he moved around in Europe and stayed at gastronomic hot spots, at the world exhibition in Vienna, on the French Riviera, in San Remo, and also in Switzerland, where Ritz became the director of the Grand Hôtel National in Lucerne in 1877.

The period of the fin de siècle was also a happy-go-lucky time characterized by a love of display and decadence. Ritz was a stage manager for that world theater. He succeeded in building up a new type of luxury hotel business which left nothing to be desired. His collaboration with Auguste Escoffier, whom he first hired in Monte Carlo in 1884, began in the 1880s. In the nineteenth century, there was no lack of outstanding chefs. But Escoffier was without a doubt the most important chef at that time, a creative mind with a great deal of entrepreneurial spirit, but also a person with distinctive staying power and a penchant for strict systems. After Ritz became the general manager of the Savoy Hotel in London in 1889, the hotel rapidly developed into one of the most important in the world; as of 1890, Escoffier was responsible for the kitchen. Many of Escoffier's most well-known dishes, often named after people who were hotel guests at the Savoy, originated in those years. For example, *Pêche Melba*, a peeled peach poached in syrup upon a layer of vanilla ice cream and coated with a raspberry purée, calls to mind the well-known singer Nellie Melba, who appeared at the London Royal Opera House from 1892 to 1893.

When Ritz still managed the Savoy Hotel in London, he began to found a hotel business under his own name, which led to Ritz and Escoffier being dismissed from the Savoy in the end. Ritz was accused of being responsible for the disappearance of wine and spirits. Escoffier was charged with having received bribes from suppliers. In 1898, Ritz opened the famous Hôtel Ritz, with its 210 rooms, on the Place Vendôme in Paris. The French entrepreneur Louis-Alexandre Marnier-Lapostolle helped him with buying the hotel. Marnier-Lapostolle was the producer of a liqueur made of bitter orange and cognac. Oranges were an exotic and expensive fruit at that time. Ritz made two contributions to the success of the drink. He introduced it during his time at the Savoy in London and the name Grand Marnier, which is used to this day, also comes from him.

With his new hotel on the Place Vendôme, Ritz set new standards for the luxury hotel business. In retrospect, we might smile about some of them. Hygiene was a big topic at that time. Ritz accommodated the zeitgeist by having hotel rooms fitted out with a private bathroom. The rooms were luxuriously furnished in the style of different eras. The china, cutlery, and crystal were of the most luxurious kind available at that time. Escoffier brought along a big part of his kitchen staff from London. His kitchen brigade was virtually organized in a military fashion, which made an extensive menu possible. At that time, it was still unusual to come into a restaurant, to decide on a dish right there, and then to be served quickly, too. The Ritz attracted chic society like a magnet and created a world of its own, which Marcel Proust brilliantly described in his work *A la recherche du temps perdu* (Remembrance of Things Past).

At heart, César Ritz was more of an entrepreneur than a hotelier. He constantly advanced further projects. In 1905, he opened the Ritz Hotel in London as a competitor to the Savoy, which had thrown him out. In the years that followed, further Ritz Hotels were added in Madrid, New York, Johannesburg, Cairo and Montreal. The Ritz Hotels were not a true hotel chain. The financing came from different investors. Ritz himself gave his name and the reputation connected with it, and he started the operation rolling.

From 1902 on, César Ritz's state of health rapidly deteriorated. His wife, Marie-Louise, and his son, Charles Ritz, continued to run the business. Ritz died in 1918 and was buried in his birthplace. The reputation of his hotels has long outlived him.

Purée Crécy
Cream of Carrot Soup

Serves 4

> *4 tablespoons butter*
> *6 medium carrots, peeled and chopped*
> *1 medium onion, chopped*
> *Salt and white pepper to taste*
> *Pinch of sugar*
> *1 quart chicken stock*
> *½ cup rice, uncooked*
> *¾ cup heavy cream*

Melt 2 tablespoons of butter in a saucepan and add the onions, carrots, salt, white pepper and sugar and cook on medium heat until vegetables are soft, about 6 minutes.

Add the remaining butter. Add the stock and rice and bring to a boil. Reduce the heat to medium low and simmer until the rice and carrots are very tender, about 25-30 minutes.

Transfer the soup to a blender and carefully blend it until smooth and creamy. Return the soup to the pan and bring to a boil. Add more chicken stock if the soup is too thick. Reduce the heat to low and add the cream and mix to combine. Remove the pan from the heat and add 2 tablespoons of butter and whisk it into the soup until melted. Serve the soup with buttered croutons.

Salade Irma

Salade Irma is a 1906 recipe from the Hôtel Ritz in Paris created by its famous chef, Auguste Escoffier.

Serves 4

> *12 asparagus tips, blanched*
> *¼ lb. French green beans, blanched and cut into 1 inch pieces*
> *½ lb. cauliflower, blanched and cut into small florets*
> *1 baby cucumber, thinly sliced*
> *2 radishes, thinly sliced*
> *2 cups fresh frisée lettuce, washed and picked (use the young*
> *yellow part in the center)*
> *½ teaspoon fresh lemon juice*
> *1 ½ teaspoons extra virgin olive oil*
> *Edible flowers*
> *2 tablespoons mayonnaise*
> *2 tablespoons heavy cream*
> *1 teaspoon lemon juice*
> *1 teaspoon Dijon mustard*
> *½ teaspoon salt*
> *½ teaspoon black pepper*
> *1 tablespoon chopped fresh tarragon*

To make the dressing, whisk the last 7 ingredients together in a bowl to combine.

Mix the first 4 ingredients together in a bowl and add the dressing (to taste).

In a separate bowl, add the frisée and dress with lemon juice, olive oil and salt and pepper to taste.

To plate, put 3 asparagus on each plate and a mound of the other vegetables on top. Place the frisée salad on top of the vegetables and some edible flowers on top of the salad. Decorate the plate with slices of radish.

TOURNEDOS RACHEL

The life of Elisa-Rachel Félix was like a shooting star. She came from the streets of Paris and was the most famous French actress for a short time. Rachel was born in 1821 in a tavern in Switzerland when her parents were touring artists. A large number of foods bear her name, including a consommé, an egg dish, sweetbreads, a filet of sole, and chicken medaillons, the once famous tournedos beef marrow, and artichoke bottoms. The original recipe comes from Escoffier when he worked for Ritz. Today Elisa-Rachel Félix and the dishes named after her are forgotten.

Serves 4

>*4 filet mignon medaillons*
>*2 tablespoons olive oil*
>*4 slices beef marrow*
>*4 artichoke bottoms*
>*2 cups chicken stock*
>*Bordelaise sauce (recipe follows)*
>*12 asparagus tips*
>*Salt and pepper*

Season filets mignons with salt and pepper on both sides. Add the olive oil to a frying pan on high heat until it starts smoking lightly. Add the medaillons and cook them for 3 minutes on each side to a rare doneness. Cook longer if you want it a little more cooked. Take the medaillons from the pan and let them rest, covered with aluminum foil.

Poach the artichoke bottoms in salted chicken stock until tender.

Season the pieces of marrow and briefly sear them on both sides in a hot sauté pan.

Blanch the asparagus in salted boiling water for 30 seconds and immediately immerse them in an ice bath to stop the cooking. Drain them and pat dry and briefly sauté them in butter. Season with salt and pepper.

Arrange the filets on the plates and top each with a cooked artichoke bottom. Put one piece of marrow in each artichoke cavity and pour the Bordelaise sauce over the top. Garnish each plate with 3 asparagus tips.

BORDELAISE SAUCE

> *2 tablespoons and 1 teaspoon butter*
> *2 shallots, finely diced*
> *Bouquet garni (thyme, bay leaf, parsley stalks, black peppercorn)*
> *1 cup red wine*
> *2 cups veal stock*
> *Salt and pepper*

Sauté the shallots in a half tablespoon of butter on medium low heat until soft. Add the red wine and cook to reduce until it's almost all gone. Add veal stock and bouquet garni and simmer until it's been reduced to half and has thickened. Remove the bouquet garni and season with salt and pepper. Add the rest of the butter and stir until the butter has melted into the sauce.

FRAISES À LA RITZ

Serves 4

> *2 cups fresh strawberries*
> *1 tablespoon sugar*
> *1 tablespoon Grand Marnier*

Halve strawberries and place them in a shallow bowl with sugar and Grand Marnier. Chill for 30 minutes.

BERRY CREAM SAUCE

> *½ cup fresh strawberries*
> *2 tablespoons powdered sugar*
> *1/2 cup heavy cream*
> *1/2 teaspoon vanilla extract*

Purée the strawberries in a blender until smooth. Transfer to a bowl and add 1 tablespoon of powdered sugar. Chill for 30 minutes.

Whip the cream until nearly stiff and add 1 tablespoon of powdered sugar and vanilla and continue whipping the cream until stiff.

Gradually fold purée into the whipped cream and fold in another tablespoon of powdered sugar if desired.

Spoon sauce over halved strawberries in a bowl and garnish with some mint.

Serve immediately.

OSCAR OF THE WALDORF

Oscar Tschirky's life and career sound like a story that is too good to be true, the story of a poor man who attained prestige and wealth in America through his great commitment. Oscar Tschirky was the maître d'hôtel of the Waldorf=Astoria for fifty years, from its opening in 1893 until 1943. The famous hotel owes its reputation to him to a large extent. But let us start at the beginning.

Oscar Tschirky was born in La Chaux-de-Fonds in 1866. His parents came from the German-speaking part of Switzerland. Oscar began his schooling in La Chaux-de-Fonds and later he and his brother Brutus were sent to Fribourg to work on a farm. His brother, who was ten years older, soon emigrated to the United States. He enthusiastically wrote home about the opportunities for making money in the New World. At the age of 17, Oscar followed him. On the day before the Brooklyn Bridge opened, he arrived in New York, applied for American citizenship and began to look for work. There were no vacancies at the hotel where his brother worked. Oscar found a job as a porter at the famous Hoffman House hotel on Broadway. He went all out and quickly proved his efficiency. Soon he was no longer a porter and was assigned new tasks. Oscar Tschirky became a floor supervisor, worked at the reception desk, in the accounting department, organized parties and became a steward on the hotel owner's yacht.

On the recommendation of Oscar Wilde, in 1887 he is supposed to have been wooed away by Delmonico's, where he served at the bar, but also organized a wide variety of events. Three years later, he finally applied for the position of maître d'hôtel of the first Waldorf Hotel, which opened its doors in 1893. The hotel was built by the famous architect Henry Hardenbergh for the industrialist William Waldorf Astor. The Waldorf was a hotel palace with 450 rooms, halls, restaurants and bars.

Oscar Tschirky had the job of organizing the opening gala with two thousand guests. Magnificent events later became his trademark, recalling Vatel and Ritz in a certain sense.

Through the extraordinary dishes it offered, the Waldorf attracted a great number of prominent figures and became a hub of social activity. For special events, for instance, the ballroom was converted into a circus menagerie or into a Roman park landscape. The extravagance was often sensational. Business was so good that John Jacob Astor IV, a cousin of the builder of the first Waldorf, had an even bigger hotel, the Astoria, built right next to it. The Astoria had seventeen floors, more than 1,000 rooms, and a ballroom for 1,500 guests. Both hotels were joined by a connecting passageway, the Peacock Alley. The double hyphen (Waldorf=Astoria), which must be between the names to be correct, recalls that connecting passageway even today.

In 1929, the old Waldorf=Astoria was demolished and the Empire State Building was built at the same location as the tallest building in the world at that time. The new Waldorf=Astoria came into being further east on Park Avenue and its size was again impressive: two thousand rooms and a hundred apartments were spread over forty-seven floors. At Grand Central Terminal, the Waldorf=Astoria had its own platform with a private underground passageway used by personalities ranging from Franklin D. Roosevelt and Douglas MacArthur to George W. Bush. Oscar Tschirky organized the opening event for the new hotel as well. Meanwhile he had turned 63 years old. When the Waldorf=Astoria celebrated its 50th anniversary, it was also the 50th anniversary of the day when Oscar Tschirky started working there. Tschirky's biography, *Oscar of the Waldorf*, which seems more like an autobiography, came out for the anniversary. When Oscar Tschirky died, the flags at the Waldorf=Astoria were flown at half-mast for days. The newspapers were full of detailed obituaries. He bequeathed his estate and his collection of more than ten thousand menus to Cornell University.

Everyone called Oscar Tschirky just Oscar. In 1896, he published *The Cook Book by "Oscar" of the Waldorf*. There are several recipes bearing the name Waldorf in the cookbook: *Chicken Waldorf Style,*

Sweetbreads Waldorf, Potatoes Waldorf, Blanc-Mange Waldorf Style, Sherbet Waldorf Style, and *Welsh Rabbit Oscar Style.*

The dish that is the most well-known and widespread to this day, however, is undoubtedly the *Waldorf Salad*, a salad made from sour apples and raw celery cut into strips, with chopped walnut kernels and a light mayonnaise. Celery stalks were used in the original recipe; today it is mostly cut celery root. *Filet à la Oscar* (Filet Oscar Style), a steak with crab meat, blanched asparagus and Béarnaise Sauce, is also attributed to Oscar Tschirky. *Eggs Benedict* are poached eggs served on toast or halved English muffins with a slice of browned cooked ham or breakfast bacon and Hollandaise Sauce. Today they can be found at many breakfast buffets at international hotels. There are different opinions about the history of their exact origin. In 1942, Lemuel Benedict, a former Wall Street trader, wrote in a column in *The New Yorker* that one morning in 1894 he went to the Waldorf with a hangover and asked for buttered toast, poached eggs, baked ham and a dash of Hollandaise Sauce. Oscar Tschirky was so impressed by the order that he later put the dish on the breakfast and lunch menu; however, the ham was replaced by bacon and the toast by English muffins. Another anecdote claims that Eggs Benedict was created by Delmonico's. There would be a connection with Switzerland there, too.

OYSTER SOUP

Serves 4

> *1 dozen oysters in shells or fresh shucked jarred oysters*
> *in their juices*
> *1 oz. butter*
> *2 tablespoons flour*
> *4 cups fish stock*
> *Salt and pepper*
> *Pinch of ground nutmeg*

> *1 tablespoon parsley, finely chopped*
> *1 egg yolk*
> *½ tablespoon lemon juice*

Shuck the oysters and finely chop them and save their juices. Add the butter to a saucepan over medium heat and let melt, then add the flour and stir to combine. Cook the flour in the butter for 2 minutes, then gradually add the fish stock, stirring constantly until the roux dissolves into the soup and comes to a boil. Reduce the heat to low and let it cook for 15 minutes. Add the chopped oysters and strain their juices into the soup and cook for 5 minutes. Season with salt and pepper to taste and add the nutmeg and parsley. Remove the pan from the heat. Beat the egg yolk with the lemon juice and gradually add to the soup, stirring to combine. Serve the soup immediately topped with buttered croutons.

WALDORF SALAD

Serves 4

> *½ cup celery, julienned*
> *2 apples, peeled and julienned*
> *Grapes, halved*
> *2 tablespoons walnuts, toasted and chopped*
> *½ cup yogurt*
> *½ cup crème fraîche or sour cream*
> *3 teaspoons lemon juice*
> *A pinch of white pepper*
> *Salt to taste*
> *¼ cup walnut oil*

To make the dressing, combine yogurt, crème fraîche and lemon juice. Whisk the oil in slowly until emulsified. Season with salt and white pepper.

In a bowl, mix the apples, celery, grapes and walnuts. Pour the dressing and toss to coat the salad. Serve on a leaf of lettuce arranged on a plate.

CHICKEN WALDORF STYLE

Serves 4

> 1 whole chicken breast, skin on and bone in
> 1 quart cold water
> 1 teaspoon black peppercorn
> 2 bay leaves
> 1 sprig of thyme
> 1 tablespoon sea salt
> ½ small onion, finely diced
> 3 tablespoons butter
> ¼ cup white wine
> 2 cups heavy cream
> ½ tablespoon ground nutmeg
> 1 tablespoon white truffle oil
> 1 egg yolk
> 1 tablespoon Madeira wine
> Salt and pepper
> 1 tablespoon chopped parsley

In a pot, add the water, peppercorn, bay leaf, thyme and sea salt and gently bring it to a simmer and let it go for 10 minutes. Add the chicken breast to the simmering liquid and poach it for 15 minutes or until meat is cooked thoroughly (do not overcook it, it's okay if it's still a little pink in the middle).

Remove the chicken from the pot and let it cool completely. Discard the poaching liquid or save it for another use (it's a good chicken broth). Remove the skin and the bone from the breast and cut the meat into neat 1 inch dices. Reserve.

In a sauté pan, sauté the onions in 1 tablespoon of butter until cooked, about 3 minutes. Add the white wine and reduce until almost gone. Add the chicken and the cream and gently simmer until cream has thickened to a sauce consistency, about 10 minutes. Add the nutmeg and truffle oil and mix to combine.

Remove the pan from the heat. Whisk the egg yolk with the Madeira wine and slowly pour this mixture into the cream sauce, stirring constantly to integrate the egg yolk mixture into the sauce without scrambling the egg. Add 2 tablespoons of butter and stir to emulsify into the sauce. Season with salt and pepper to taste and mix in the chopped parsley.

Serve with mashed potatoes or noodles.

SHERBET WALDORF STYLE

Serves 4

> *½ lb. sugar*
> *1 cup water*
> *1 oz. raisins*
> *1 oz. dried figs, finely diced*
> *1 sachet with 6 cloves and a small cinnamon stick*
> *Food coloring, red*
> *½ cup orange juice*
> *1 tablespoon lemon juice*
> *1 cup port wine*
> *2 oz. muscatel grapes*
> *2 oz. blanched almonds*

Bring sugar and water to a boil until sugar is dissolved. Place raisins, figs and sachet in a bowl and pour over the hot sugar syrup. Let this mixture cool completely.

Strain the syrup, discarding the sachet and reserving the fruit. Add 2 drops of red food coloring into the syrup to make a delicate pink color. Add the orange juice and lemon juice and the port wine and chill this mixture in the refrigerator for at least 3 hours.

Put the chilled syrup into an ice cream maker and proceed according to manufacturer's instructions.

When the sherbet is almost done but not quite frozen yet, add the reserved raisins and figs, the grapes and blanched almonds and finish the freezing process.

Keep the sherbet in the freezer in a container with a tight lid for up to 2 weeks.

HENRY HALLER: THE WHITE HOUSE CHEF

Life in the White House is immensely fascinating to the general public. Individual presidents are remembered not only for the political achievements of their terms of office, but for their way of life and the personal style they brought to the White House. The First Lady's clothing, the changes in furnishings, the pets, the Christmas tree decorations, the china that is redesigned for each president, and especially the dishes eaten by the president's family or served to their guests are frequently observed, commented on, and evaluated.

Since there are hardly any restrictions on their choice, eating habits say a great deal about presidents. And precisely because presidents are aware that their eating habits are known throughout the country, the dishes served often provide a clue about how they want to be perceived in public. Whether they offer local American cuisine like George and Martha Washington, whether they are amateur cooks like Eisenhower, whether they invite their guests to breakfast instead of dinner to save money and even care about leftovers like Calvin Coolidge, whether they lead an extravagantly chic lifestyle like Martin van Buren and Herbert Hoover, or whether they eat as much as William Howard Taft, who weighed over 300 pounds at the end of his term of office and couldn't even climb out of a bathtub by himself anymore—all of that sends a message to the people.

Whoever goes to the White House Visitor Center today can listen to an audio recording of Henry Haller and hear about how he was hired by Lady Bird Johnson, the wife of the thirty-sixth president, in 1966 as a Swiss Executive Chef and what he later experienced working at the White House. Henry Haller clearly stands out from the list of White House chefs. He worked for five presidents altogether: Johnson, Ford, Nixon, Carter, and Reagan. Although Haller's unusually long tenure can certainly be attributed to his performance as a chef, it can also be attributed to his ability to recognize the preferences and culinary traditions of the individual presidential families and to create a special style from them, just as required by the Executive Residence Procedural Manual at that time, namely, "that the First Family menus are prepared to the highest standards and in accordance with the Family's tastes and preferences."

Haller himself came from Altdorf. He received his culinary training at the Park Hotel in Davos and later worked at the Bellevue Palace in Bern, the Grand Hotel in Bürgenstock, and at the Ritz-Carlton in Montreal, among others. As of 1953, he was employed at various American hotels, restaurants and clubs. When he applied for the position of Executive Chef at the White House, he was in charge of a team of fifty people at the Sheraton East in New York. The White House Executive Chef must master a considerable range of gastronomic skills; he must be able to prepare all kinds of meals—from breakfast for individual family members to lavish state banquets with more than a thousand guests—supremely well and perfectly. Henry Haller had that ability. Through his training and professional experience, he was shaped by French cuisine, which is particularly well suited to representation. But he also had a very good knowledge of Swiss, German, Italian, Austrian, and American cuisine. That considerable culinary range went very well with the cultural and ethnic melting pot of the USA.

After he left his job as White House Chef, Haller published his professional memoirs with many recipes in *The White House Family Cookbook*, which is far more than a cookbook. It is a miniature culinary portrait of the five presidential families Haller worked for. Through Haller's description of their eating habits, the presidents become alive and give readers a new perspective on their individual families. For that reason, reading the book is worthwhile not only for people who like recipes. It very impressively confirms Brillat-Savarin's famous quote "Tell me what you eat, and I will tell you who you are."

The family of President Johnson, who served from 1963 to 1969, came from Texas. It is hardly surprising that meat dishes, Mexican dishes like Chili con Carne and other dishes at the Johnson's ranch were also frequently served at the White House. In addition, there were dishes that can only be found in the United States such as sweet potatoes with toasted marshmallows.

During the time of President Nixon, who served from 1969 to 1974, salads, cottage cheese and lighter fare were very popular. Communal meals were very formal again, with dishes prepared according to traditional recipes. It went very well with Nixon's foreign policy that dishes from remote parts of the world were also served at the White House. Nixon was the first president to visit China; the popular pandas at the National Zoo in Washington have been there since then. One of Pat Nixon's favorite dishes was Chinese Walnut Chicken. When she described the recipe to journalists as "a favorite of Henry's," the members of the press assumed that Henry Kissinger had brought back the recipe from China. But it came from Henry Haller.

Not much is remembered about the recipes from the time of President Ford, who served from 1974 to 1977. Soups, salads and sandwiches were among their favorite dishes, as well as some family recipes for desserts. Ford became vice president during Nixon's second term and he finally became president himself after Nixon had to resign as a result of the Watergate scandal. He could never get out of Nixon's shadow. In November 1976, Ford narrowly lost the presidential election to Jimmy Carter, the Democratic candidate.

The eating habits in the White House fundamentally changed with the Carter family. After more than 120 years, the American president came from the Old South again. With him, the lifestyle from Dixieland also moved into the White House, often with simple dishes from Carter's home and with unconventional hospitality. Barbecues, which were already popular during Carter's election campaign, were also organized at the White House. The menus were now written in English instead of in French as previously. Even as president, it was important to Carter to maintain the way of life of the common man and to seem close to the people. The dishes from those years represent that desire very well.

Although the transition to the term of President Reagan, who served from 1981 to 1989, was smooth for the White House kitchen staff and domestic staff, a completely different style prevailed once again. Sophisticated taste made its entrance once more; optimism and new self-confidence could also soon be noticed in the most famous kitchen in the USA. With Ronald Reagan, many VIPs from Hollywood and show business came to the White House. Frank Sinatra, Audrey Hepburn, Charlton Heston, and Gregory Peck were among the guests. Henry Haller conjured up whatever met with approval.

Henry Haller was proud of his Swiss origin. He also brought Swiss specialties to the White House. Some of those recipes can be found in *The White House Family Cookbook*: the recipes for Rösti, Meringue, Braised Swiss Steak, Eggplant Ticinese, Swiss Gruyère Soufflé and also instructions for making a whole lot of Christmas baked goods such as Swiss Christmas Cookies, Berner Leckerli and Mailänderli.

PRESIDENT CARTER'S LENTIL AND FRANKS SOUP

Makes 3 quarts

> ½ lb. dried lentils
> 2 tablespoons butter
> 1 cup chopped onions
> 1 cup chopped scallions, white parts only
> 2 garlic cloves, finely minced
> ½ finely diced carrots
> 1 cup diced celery
> 1 bay leaf
> ½ teaspoon dried thyme
> A dash of salt
> 1/8 teaspoon freshly ground white pepper
> 1 large Idaho baking potato, peeled and finely diced
> 2 ½ quarts hot beef bouillon

4 frankfurters
1 tablespoon chopped fresh parsley

Cover lentils with cold water; let soak overnight. Drain well and discard any small stones.

In a 4-quart soup pot, melt butter; sauté onions, scallions, and garlic for 5 minutes. Do not brown.

Add diced carrots and celery, bay leaf, thyme, salt and pepper; mix well.

Cover, and simmer slowly for 10 minutes.

Add drained lentils, diced potato, and hot bouillon. Bring to a boil; set cover slightly ajar, and simmer briskly for 1 ½ hours. (To enhance flavor, add a pig's knuckle or ham bone.)

Slice franks into very thin rounds and add to soup pot; boil for 1 minute.

Just before serving, sprinkle with chopped parsley. Serve hot.

PRESIDENT JOHNSON'S CHOPPED GARDEN SALAD

Serves 6

2 cups diced iceberg lettuce
2 ripe tomatoes, peeled, seeded, and diced
1 cup diced Bermuda onion
1 cup diced green bell pepper
1 cup diced celery
1 teaspoon salt
½ teaspoon freshly ground black pepper
Juice of 2 lemons
1 teaspoon cider vinegar
1 teaspoon vegetable oil

2 large lettuce leaves

In a large mixing bowl, combine diced vegetables. Toss with salt, pepper, lemon juice, and vinegar.

Add oil and mix well. Chill.

Spoon salad onto lettuce leaves and serve at once.

PRESIDENT REAGAN'S LOBSTER MOUSSELINE

Serves 10

Two 2-pound fresh lobsters
4 tablespoons olive oil
½ cup finely minced shallots
2 garlic cloves, finely minced
1 cup chopped leeks, white part only
1 tablespoon salt
1/8 teaspoon black pepper
2 teaspoons fennel seed
½ cup warm brandy
1 cup home-made or commercial tomato sauce
1 tablespoon sweet paprika
¼ tablespoon cayenne pepper
1 cup heavy cream, hot
2 packages (½ oz.) unflavored gelatin
4 tablespoons dry sherry
2 cups heavy cream
10 thin slices of black truffle or black olive
10 thin strips of red bell pepper
10 fresh parsley springs
10 thin slices of lemon

Remove stomach and crack claws of each lobster.

In a large sauté pan, heat oil over medium-high heat, add whole lobsters and sauté until shells turn red.

Add shallots, garlic, leeks, salt, pepper, and fennel seed; sauté for 7 to 8 minutes.

Pour in warm brandy and flame carefully, using a long match; let flames die out.

Cover and simmer over medium heat for 5 minutes.

Stir in tomato sauce, paprika, cayenne pepper, and hot cream.

Cover, and simmer 5 minutes more.

Transfer lobsters to a casserole dish and refrigerate (to make removal of meat from the shells easier).

Reduce the lobster broth over medium-high heat to about 1 cup. Remove from heat and pour into a food processor.

Remove lobster meat from the shells; chop fine and add to food processor.

Purée lobster meat with broth for 3 minutes until very smooth.

In the top of a double boiler, dissolve gelatin in sherry. Add to the lobster purée, and blend for 10 seconds.

Transfer mixture to a large mixing bowl. In a clean, cold bowl, whip the cream until stiff and fold in.

Pour into a 1½-quart ring mold, filling to ½ inch form the top. Smooth the surface.

Refrigerate several hours or overnight.

Immerse mold briefly in hot water, then turn out onto a serving platter.

Decorate top with alternating truffle or olive slices and red pepper strips.

Garnish platter with alternating fresh parsley springs and lemon slices.

Serve at once with chilled creamy horseradish sauce and slices of herbed French bread.

CREAMY HORSERADISH SAUCE

Makes 2 cups

1 cup sour cream
½ cup mayonnaise
½ cup freshly grated horseradish
A pinch of salt
1 teaspoon Worcestershire sauce

In a small mixing bowl, combine sour cream with mayonnaise.

Fold in horseradish. Season with salt and Worcestershire sauce.

Spoon into a glass bowl. Refrigerate until serving time.

PRESIDENT FORD'S CHICKEN CORDON BLEU

Serves 6

Six 6-ounce chicken breasts, boned and skinned
2 tablespoons butter
2 tablespoons flour
¾ cup hot milk
¼ teaspoon salt
A pinch of freshly ground white pepper
A pinch of nutmeg
6 tablespoons finely diced Gruyère cheese
4 tablespoons finely diced cooked ham
1 tablespoon chopped fresh parsley
½ cup flour
2 eggs, beaten with a pinch of salt and white pepper
2 cups fresh French bread crumbs
½ cup clarified butter
Fresh parsley springs

From each chicken breast, remove the small fillet. Wrap the small fillets in aluminum foil and flatten by pounding with a wooden mallet.

Use a sharp knife to cut a pocket in each chicken breast: On each side of the indentation left from the small fillet, make a long slit about ¼-inch deep (do not pierce through breast); gently pull the center strip away from the breast to reveal the pocket.

In a saucepan, melt butter over low heat, add flour, and work into a roux. Cook for two minutes, stirring constantly.

Stir in hot milk, salt, pepper, and nutmeg, and bring to a boil. Cook over low heat, stirring, until very thick; let cool.

When sauce is almost cold, fold in diced cheese and ham and chopped parsley.

Divide evenly among the chicken breast pockets. Press a flattened fillet over each stuffed pocket.

Carefully roll each stuffed breast in flour, dip in beaten egg mixture, and gently roll in fresh bread crumbs.

Transfer chicken breasts to a casserole dish. Refrigerate for 1 hour.

Preheat *oven to 375° F.*

In a cast-iron skillet, heat clarified butter over medium-high heat; sauté chicken breasts, stuffed side down, until golden brown. Carefully turn to brown other side.

Return sautéed chicken breasts to casserole dish. Bake in preheated oven for 10 minutes.

Arrange on a serving platter and garnish with springs of parsley. Serve at once, with a rice salad and a hot green vegetable.

Mrs. Nixon's Florida Lime Pie

Makes a 9-inch pie

1 cup sugar
¼ teaspoon salt
1 package (¼ oz.) unflavored gelatin
¼ cup water
½ cup lime juice
4 egg yolks
1 teaspoon grated lime rind
4 egg whites, at room temperature
1 fully baked 9-inch pie crust
Sweet whipped cream

In the top of a double boiler, combine ½ cup sugar with the salt, gelatin, and water.

In a small bowl, combine the lime juice with the egg yolks; stir into the gelatin mixture in the double boiler, using a wire whisk.

Cook for about 7 minutes, or until gelatin dissolves and mixture thickens.

Remove from heat and stir in the lime rind.

Place pan in a bowl of ice water, stirring occasionally as mixture cools.

In a large clean, dry bowl, beat egg whites until stiff; gradually add the remaining ½ cup of sugar, beating constantly.

Fold cooled lime mixture into stiff egg white, using a plastic spatula.

Turn into prebaked pie shell and refrigerate for several hours, or until set. Cover pie with sweet whipped cream and keep refrigerated until serving time.

JULIUS MAGGI: SOUP IN
THE INDUSTRIAL AGE

No other Swiss citizen has had such a profound impact on the cultural history of soup as Julius Maggi, the well-known pioneer in industrial food production. We have Maggi to thank for many innovative products that make it possible to prepare inexpensive, healthy and tasty dishes for the average household.

Julius Maggi was born in Frauenfeld in 1846 as a child of Italian immigrants. He had that entrepreneurial spirit that has remained characteristic of many second-generation immigrants in Switzerland to this day. As a mill owner and businessman, Maggi's father had already earned a considerable fortune. Julius Maggi was only twenty-three years old when he took over his father's business in Kemptthal near Winterthur. It was a semi-industrial business which Julius Maggi expanded with additional mills and vegetable gardening operations in the years to come.

Julius Maggi was more than an entrepreneur who precisely observed the market, he also pursued social concerns. With his colleague Fridolin Schuler, Maggi developed inexpensive protein-rich legume products. As a flavor enhancement, Maggi seasoning sauce came into being while he was working on soup concentrates in 1886. The product was a big success and is still on the market throughout the world today. Maggi seasoning sauce has a flavor very similar to lovage, but it does not contain any lovage. Paradoxically lovage is now also called the Maggi herb.

A groundbreaking success was the launching of the Maggi bouillon cube (Kub). Maggi actually wanted to have the cube patented as Cub. But that name was considered to be too general to be able to be protected. That is why he chose the spelling Kub and founded the Société du Bouillon Kub. In 1912, six million of those bouillon cubes were sold in France each month. Paris was virtually inundated with bouillon cube advertisements. Free bouillon samples were given out in street kitchens; walls were full of enamel signs with advertising labels; sandwich men carrying Kub billboards on their bellies and backs appeared everywhere; entire armies of cyclists with advertising labels rode on their way. Maggi owed his success not only to the quality of the product, but also to modern marketing and proactive advertising methods.

Interestingly enough, cubism originated as a new art movement at exactly the same time. While Maggi compressed soup concentrate into a cube, an entire art movement abstracted reality into cubes and into other geometric shapes. The first important book about cubism, *Du Cubisme* by Albert Gleizes and Jean Metzinger, was published in 1912 and reproduced cubist paintings by both authors, but also by Cézanne, Léger, Juan Gris, Francis Picabia, Marcel Duchamp, Picasso, Braque, André Derain, and Marie Laurencin. In the same year, Picasso painted his *Paysage aux affiches*, where a Maggi cube can be seen.

In the very same year, 1912, Maggi unexpectedly died of a stroke. In France, his company was soon drawn deeper and deeper into the whirlpool of nationalist hostilities, which were characteristic of the period directly before World War I. The Action française, a right-wing and later openly fascist movement, had already trained its sights on the pasteurized milk business beforehand. Maggi was suspected of being a German company and pursuing German interests. When World War I broke out in August 1914, the Maggi laboratory in France and most of the more than 800 delivery stations were destroyed. The well-known enamel signs with the advertising labels were torn off walls. Rumors circulated that the company was spying for Germany. According to one of the conspiracy theories, the purpose of the Maggi enamel signs was even to indicate roads for the German troops to march through. Of course, they were all fantasies.

In the period after World War I, the Maggi company sought cooperation with Auguste Escoffier, the famous French chef who worked with César Ritz. There has frequently been speculation about the cooperation. In fact, there are papers by Escoffier in which he comments on Maggi products he experimented with. The Maggi cube and many other of Julius Maggi's products are still on grocery store shelves throughout the world.

These three soup recipes come from the once widely circulated cookbook *Hundert Küchenspezialitäten aus allen Kantonen* (One Hundred Culinary Specialties from All the Cantons), which was published in several editions by Maggi's food plant in Kemptthal in the 1940s. Below the recipe, it was always indicated that the soup was also available in a ready-to-serve pouch from Maggi's soup product line.

SCHOPPA DA JOTTA: ENGADINE BARLEY SOUP (GRISONS)

1 lb. smoked beef, also some fresh meat if desired
5 oz. barley
1 small cabbage, chopped (also white beans if desired)
½ lb. potatoes, cut into medium dices or cubes
1 tablespoon flour
3 tablespoons heavy cream or half and half cream

Put the meat and barley (and white beans if used) into a pot filled with 7 cups of cold water and bring to a boil, then reduce the heat to medium and cook for two hours until the meat is soft (add more water as needed).

Add the cabbage and potatoes and cook for another hour or until the vegetables are soft.

Mix the flour with the cream and stir to dissolve, making sure there are no lumps of flour and add to the soup and stir to combine. Cook for a few minutes until the soup has thickened, then season to taste and enhance by adding a little Maggi soup seasoning before serving.

MINESTRONE (TICINO)

All seasonal vegetables, in any case:

> *2 to 4 carrots*
> *1 celery root*
> *1 leek*
> *1 tomato*
> *1 small cabbage*
> *2 to 3 potatoes*
> *1 clove of garlic*
> *1 onion*
> *1 bay leaf*
> *Some peppercorns*
> *¼ cup bacon*
> *1 handful of rice*
> *1 handful of white beans*
> *1 handful of pasta*
> *2 Maggi bouillon cubes*
> *Grated cheese*

Wash the vegetables and cut them up and roast them with the bacon until they are golden brown. Put all the vegetables, including the white beans softened by soaking in water the night before, and the spices into 10 cups of water and let simmer for 1½ hours. Then add the pasta, rice and bouillon cubes and cook the soup for another 30 minutes. Serve with grated cheese.

BASEL FLOUR SOUP

> *2 oz. butter or fat*
> *3½ oz. flour*
> *2 Maggi bouillon cubes*
> *2 oz. grated cheese*

7 cups water
Salt to taste

Heat up the butter or fat in a big flat cast-iron pot and add the flour and stir continuously until browned but not burned. Then immediately stir in the water, pouring a little bit at a time and stirring to combine after each addition, then add the bouillon cubes and cook the moderately thick soup for approximately 30 minutes on low heat. Season the soup to taste with salt. Put half of the cheese into a soup tureen and strain the soup through a fine sieve over the cheese. Serve the other half of the cheese on the side.

SAVORY SWISS SOUPS AND THEIR STORIES

Soup was the first nourishment cavemen took from the cooking pot. Soups were the overture to sumptuous dinners during the *Belle Époque* and soup has remained an object of culinary invention and zeal to this day. The soups in this chapter tell stories about Switzerland.

POTAGE À LA GUILLAUME TELL

Wilhelm Tell is the legendary Swiss national hero. He was a freedom fighter who resisted and eventually killed Gessler, the malicious Habsburg bailiff. The best-known episode about him is when Gessler forced him to use his crossbow to shoot an apple off the head of his son, Walter. That is why most of the dishes named after him contain apples. But that is not the case with *Potage à la Guillaume Tell*. The soup contains meatballs made from wild game instead. Hunting game was reserved for the nobility and common people such as Wilhelm Tell were denied that privilege in the Middle Ages. As the murderer of a tyrant, Tell would certainly not have respected that rule and would have thoroughly enjoyed eating the meatballs.

Potage à la Guillaume Tell was created by Ferdinando Grandi, one of the great nineteenth-century chefs. When creating the soup, perhaps he had Rossini's beautiful opera *Guillaume Tell* in mind.

Serves 4

DUCK PURÉE

> *1 duck leg quarter, cooked (Duck confit preferable)*
> *2 shallots, sliced*
> *1 garlic clove, chopped*
> *1 tablespoon thyme*
> *1 tablespoon butter*
> *¼ teaspoon red pepper flakes*
> *Salt and pepper to taste*
> *¼ cup white wine*
> *¼ cup heavy cream*

Remove the duck meat from the bones and shred it. Sauté the shallots in butter until soft and add the shredded duck meat, thyme and red pepper flakes and cook for about two minutes. Add the white wine and reduce until almost dry. Season with salt and pepper to taste. Transfer the duck mixture to a blender and add the cream. Blend everything to a very smooth paste. Pass the duck paste through a fine sieve into a pan and heat it on low heat. Keep warm.

BARLEY PURÉE

> *2 cups chicken stock*
> *½ cup barley*
> *2 tablespoons butter*
> *1 egg yolk*
> *Salt and pepper to taste*

Cook the barley in chicken stock until very soft. Strain the barley and save the liquid. Put the cooked barley and the butter into a blender and blend until smooth. Add a little of the reserved liquid if the purée is too thick. Add the egg yolk and quickly blend to combine. Season with salt and pepper to taste. Keep warm.

Just before serving, mix the two purées together and add some game meatballs.

ANNA WECKER'S ALMOND AND PEA SOUP

The original recipe for *Almond and Pea Soup* was published in *Ein Köstlich new Kochbuch* (A Delightful New Cookbook).

Serves 4

    1 tablespoon butter
    ½ small onion, chopped
    ½ small leek, chopped
    1 pinch of red pepper flakes
    2 cups almond milk
    2 cups water
    2 cups frozen peas, blanched
    2 tablespoons Malvoisier (or any other sweet wine)
    Salt and pepper to taste
    Cayenne pepper

On medium heat, add the butter and melt it, then sauté the onions and leeks. Add the red pepper flakes and the almond milk. Cook on low heat until the leeks and onions are soft.

Blanch the frozen peas in salted boiling water for 5 minutes. Add ¾ of the peas into the boiling almond milk and reserve the rest, keeping it warm.

Transfer the mixture to a blender and blend until smooth, then strain it into a clean pot.

Warm the soup on low heat, add 2 tablespoons of sweet white wine and season with salt and pepper to taste.

Serve the soup in warm bowls. Add the reserved peas to each bowl and sprinkle with some cayenne pepper on top.

ZANZARELLI

Zanzarelli is a well-known soup that became widespread in southern Switzerland and Italy. The recipe is a slight adaptation of Maestro Martino's fifteenth-century original recipe.

Serves 6

> *8 cups chicken broth*
> *8 eggs*
> *2 cups parmesan cheese*
> *1 cup breadcrumbs*
> *Saffron threads*
> *Cinnamon*
> *Ginger powder*
> *Ground nutmeg*
> *Pepper*

Beat together the eggs, parmesan cheese, and breadcrumbs until you have a fine, running dough.

Boil the chicken broth. As soon as it boils, reduce the heat and let simmer. Add the saffron and simmer until the broth has a nice golden color. Boil again and add the prepared dough. Whisk continuously and let boil until the dough and the broth separate.

The soup will have a grainy consistency. Take the soup off the heat and season with cinnamon, ginger powder, ground nutmeg, and pepper to taste before serving.

TOMATO SOUP FIORENTINA

The Pontifical Swiss Guard is responsible for the safety of the Pope and the security of the Apostolic Palace in Rome. Established in 1506 under Pope Julius II, the Swiss Guard is among the oldest military units in continuous operation. The Guard is best known for its Renaissance appearance with traditional weapons. But today the Guard's nonceremonial roles as security personnel and bodyguards for the Pope are significant. Swiss Guard recruits are unmarried Swiss Catholic men between 19 and 30 years of age who have completed basic military training with the Swiss Armed Forces.

Tomato Soup Fiorentina is a recipe from the 2016 edition of *The Vatican Cookbook by the Pontifical Swiss Guard.*

Serves 4

> *1 medium onion, minced*
> *1 lb. cherry tomatoes, chopped*
> *3 tablespoons olive oil*
> *2 teaspoons raw cane sugar*
> *¼ cup white balsamic vinegar*
> *1½ cups tomato juice*
> *1 cup vegetable broth*
> *2 teaspoons basil oil*
> *Fresh basil*
> *Sea salt*
> *Fresh ground black pepper*
> *4 slices of white bread, lightly toasted*
> *2 tablespoons butter*
> *1 teaspoon fresh rosemary*

SOUP

Mince the onion, chop the cherry tomatoes, and sauté in the olive oil over medium heat. Sprinkle in the sugar and let caramelize. Add the white balsamic vinegar. Pour in the tomato juice and vegetable bouillon, cover and let the soup simmer on low for 30 minutes.

Purée the soup in a blender to a smooth consistency and then strain it through a fine mesh strainer or cheese cloth. Season the tomato soup with sea salt, pepper and basil oil.

CROUTONS

Remove the crusts from the slices of lightly toasted bread and cut into small ½ inch cubes. Melt the butter in a frying pan and toast the bread until golden brown. Season the croutons with salt and fresh rosemary.

Add the croutons to the soup immediately before serving.

KAPPELER MILCHSUPPE

The First Kappel War in 1529 was an armed conflict between the Protestants and the Catholics of the Old Swiss Confederation during the Reformation. It ended without any battle having been fought. While the negotiations were going on, the soldiers of the two armies prepared a huge amount of milk soup and shared it with each other as a sign of reconciliation. Over time *Kappeler Milchsuppe* became a symbol of peaceful understanding, and the soup was later revived in critical periods of Swiss history.

The original sixteenth-century recipe is not known and perhaps never existed in writing. The recipe below was used in 2006 when the Cantons of Zurich and St. Gallen agreed on the restitution of the cultural assets taken by Zurich in 1712 during the very last conflict of the Reformation. Sometimes it takes time to resolve a disagreement, but it presented another opportunity to prepare *Kappeler Milchsuppe*.

Serves 4

> *2½ cups whole milk*
> *½ teaspoon salt*
> *1 pinch of ground nutmeg*
> *1 bay leaf*
> *1 clove*
> *4 egg yolks*
> *½ cup cream*
> *4 thick slices of white bread, cut into cubes*

Add the spices and the milk to a pan and bring to a boil. Keep on simmering.

In the meantime, beat the egg yolks and cream together to a foamy consistency.

While continuously mixing, slowly add the boiling milk to the egg yolk and cream mixture until combined.

Season the soup with salt and pepper to taste, and serve in a soup tureen.

Toast the bread in butter and add to the soup immediately before serving.

Traditionally, everyone eats out of the same soup tureen and is only allowed to eat the bread on their side.

JENATSCH'S CHRISTMAS SOUP

For many people in the Grisons, Jürg Jenatsch, who lived from 1596 to 1639, is a great freedom hero. He was a pastor, a politician, and the leader of the troops of the Grisons in the Thirty Years' War. In 1639, Jürg Jenatsch became the victim of a conspiracy and was killed with a hatchet during the carnival. Novels, plays and movies have been devoted to his colorful and sometimes obscure life.

The Camanna Jenatsch is named after him. Among all the Swiss Alpine Club huts in the Grisons, it is the one highest up in the mountains.

Jenatsch's Christmas Soup is an original recipe from the hut and definitely the right soup to buoy up exhausted hikers and mountain climbers.

Serves 4

3 tablespoons butter
1 cup onions, chopped
1⅓ cups carrots, chopped
1½ cups savoy cabbage, chopped
1 teaspoon fresh dill, chopped
2 teaspoons chives, chopped
1 pinch of cardamom
¼ cup oats
5 cups water
2½ concentrated bouillon cubes
Salt and pepper to taste
Garlic powder
½ cup cream
Whipped cream
Dill, chopped
Chives, chopped
Parsley, chopped

Heat the butter in a frying pan. As soon as it is hot, add the vegetables (including dill, chives and cardamom). Steam the vegetables and add the oats and cook over low heat for approximately 10 minutes.

In the meantime, boil the water, add the bouillon and then add the steamed vegetables and oats. Bring to a boil, season, reduce the heat and simmer for 30 minutes.

Before serving, mix in the cream and serve garnished with whipped cream and chopped herbs on top.

SWISS ARMY POT-AU-FEU

Stews are as old as military service. They are perfect for big numbers of people, can easily be kept warm, and are rather simple to prepare and to eat. For generations, Swiss soldiers have developed their own relationship to pot-au-feu. To many, the smell of pot-au-feu brings back memories of bygone experiences in nature and camaraderie.

This is an original recipe used by the Swiss military. The recipe has not changed much since the last century.

Serves 4

>   *5 cups beef stock*
>   *4 cloves*
>   *1 bay leaf*
>   *1½ lb. beef stew*
>   *3 oz. onions, large dices*
>   *8½ oz. carrots, large dices*
>   *4 oz. celery stalks, large dices*
>   *4 oz. celery root, large dices*
>   *6½ oz. savoy cabbage, large dices*
>   *4 oz. leeks, large dices*
>   *1½ lb. potatoes, large dices*
>   *½ cup parsley, chopped*
>   *Salt and pepper to taste*

Bring the beef stock and the spices to a boil. Add the beef and cook on low heat for an hour. Skim the scum off to remove the impurities. Add the vegetables and cook until just soft. Season with salt and pepper to taste and serve.

POTAGE SUISSE SERVED AT DELMONICO'S IN NEW YORK

Swiss Soup is from Alessandro Filippini's *The International Cook Book* published in New York in 1911.

Serves 6

> 2 lb. piece of beef short ribs, bone in
> 1 beef bone marrow
> 5 quarts cold water
> 1 tablespoon salt
> 2 medium carrots
> 2 white turnips
> 2 onions
> 2 celery stalks
> 2 leeks, washed clean
>
> 3 sprigs of parsley, chopped
> 1 sprig of chervil, chopped
> 1 garlic clove, crushed
>
> 4 oz. raw rice
> 2 oz. Swiss cheese or Parmesan cheese

Tie the short ribs with a string and place in a large pot with a small beef marrow bone. Pour in five quarts of cold water with a tablespoon of salt. Heat on the range and let slowly come to a boil. Skim fat from surface, then add two medium carrots, two white turnips, two onions and two celery stalks. Cover pan and let simmer at the corner of the range for two hours. Finely slice two leeks, add them to the soup and slowly boil half an hour longer. Remove the beef, carrots, turnips, onions and celery from the soup. Chop together three sprigs of fresh parsley, one sprig of chervil, and one garlic clove. Add the hash to the soup with four ounces of raw rice, lightly mix and continually simmer on low for forty minutes. Skim fat from surface of soup, transfer it to a soup tureen and serve with two ounces of grated Swiss or Parmesan cheese, separately.

CONSOMMÉ DIPLOMATE

Consommé diplomate was served at the Ritz Hotels in the Belle Époque.

Serves 4

CONSOMMÉ

> *1 carrot, chopped*
> *1 leek, chopped*
> *1 ½ chicken breasts*
> *½ onion*
> *3 egg whites*
> *1 teaspoon pepper corns*
> *3 sprigs of thyme*
> *2 bay leaves*
> *Salt*
> *1 quart chicken stock*

SAUSAGE

> 2 chicken breasts, fat removed
> 1 shallot, finely minced, sautéed in butter
> 1 carrot, finely minced, blanched
> 1 pinch of nutmeg
> Salt and pepper to taste
> 1 egg white
> Crayfish butter to taste

CRAYFISH BUTTER

> 1 shallot, chopped
> 4 oz. butter, softened
> 1 pinch of red pepper flakes
> Fresh thyme and tarragon

3 oz. crayfish

CONSOMMÉ

To clarify the chicken stock, whisk the egg whites until foamy and add the very finely chopped vegetables and herbs and mix all together. Add this mixture to the cold chicken stock in a large pot and bring to a boil on high heat, stirring continuously. Once the draft comes up to the top of the pot, reduce the heat to very low and simmer for 1 hour. Remove the pot from the heat and let it sit for about 15 minutes. With a ladle, very carefully remove the clear broth from the pot, making sure none of the egg white draft is picked up, and strain the broth into a clean pot through a thick layer of cheesecloth that is set on a fine sieve. Keep the consommé warm.

SAUSAGE

In a food processor, process the chicken breast until very smooth. Add the egg white and continue processing for about 1 minute. Add the cream and process for another minute until all is combined. Pass the chicken paste through a fine sieve into a chilled bowl. Add a little salt and pepper.

To test the sausage for seasoning, have a small pan on the stove with a little boiling water and drop in a small amount of the chicken paste and cook for a few seconds until thoroughly cooked and taste it. Add more seasoning if needed, and continue testing until you reach the desired seasoning.

Add the blanched carrots and sautéed shallots to the chicken mixture and add a pinch of nutmeg. Fold everything together with a rubber spatula.

With a spoon or a piping bag, place the chicken paté on a cling film and roll it up to form a thin log. Wrap it tightly and secure the ends. Wrap the log up in aluminum foil and poach it in simmering water for approximately 10 minutes or until cooked thoroughly. Do not overcook it or you will end up with a grainy sausage rather than a smooth sausage.

CRAYFISH BUTTER

Sauté the shallots in a little butter until soft and add the red pepper flakes, thyme, tarragon and crayfish. Cook for about 2 minutes. Let the mixture cool and then place in a food processor with 4 oz. of soft butter and process until all is smoothly combined. Transfer the butter into a container with a lid and refrigerate.

Gently sauté the sausages in crayfish butter until warm and nicely slice them. Add the sausage slices to a soup tureen and fill up with the chicken consommé. Garnish with chives, lemon juice to taste, and black truffle shaves.

LOBSTER BISQUE WALDORF

The elegant Lobster Bisque is a recipe from *The Cook Book by "Oscar" of the Waldorf* published in 1896.

Serves 4

> *1 lobster*
> *3 small carrots, chopped*
> *1 celery stalk, chopped*
> *½ onion, chopped*
> *2 garlic cloves, crushed*
> *1 tablespoon tarragon, chopped*
> *1 tablespoon butter*
> *1 lemon*
> *¼ cup cognac*
> *2 tablespoons flour*

Fill a large pot big enough to fit a whole lobster with water and bring to a boil. Add about 2 tablespoons of salt to the water. Add the lobster to the boiling water for 4–6 minutes, depending on size. Shock it in a bucket of ice water. Separate the meat from the shells. Save the coral and let it dry in an oven on very low heat for about an hour.

Put the shells in a pan with enough water to cover the shells, cook them for 30 minutes.

Discard the hard shells from the claws. Add the soft shells to a blender along with the broth and blend on high for 1 minute (work in batches). Strain the liquid using a fine sieve and press the solids with a ladle to obtain as much liquid as possible. Discard the shells and reserve the broth.

In the meantime, sauté the vegetables in the butter until the vegetables are caramelized. Deglaze with ¼ cup cognac and let reduce. Add 2 tablespoons of flour while continuously stirring for 3 minutes. Add the reserved lobster stock and simmer for 30 minutes on low.

Blend everything together until smooth. Strain through a fine sieve. Bring it back to the heat and add some cream to taste and continue cooking on low to a soup consistency.

Chop the lobster meat, sauté with butter, fresh tarragon, and lemon zest.

Put the lobster meat in a soup bowl. Add the hot bisque and garnish with the finely ground, dried coral and some drops of lemon juice.

PRESIDENT REAGAN'S HAMBURGER SOUP

President Reagan's Hamburger Soup is a dish many people have heard of, but only a few have tasted. Hamburger Soup was often served to President Reagan as a light lunch when he worked in the Oval Office. Henry Haller included the recipe in *The White House Family Cookbook*, which he published in 1987.

Serves 4

> ¼ *cup butter*
> 2 *lb. lean ground beef*
> 2 *cups onions, diced*
> 4 *garlic cloves*
> 1½ *cups carrots, diced*
> 2 *cups celery, diced*
> 1 *cup green bell pepper, diced*
> 3 *quarts hot beef broth*
> 4 *large ripe tomatoes or a 14½ oz. can of stewed tomatoes*
> ½ *teaspoon freshly ground black pepper*
> 2 *bay leaves*
> 1 *can (15 oz.) hominy*
> 2 *tablespoons parsley, chopped*

Melt the butter in a heavy skillet, add meat and brown quickly over high heat. Add diced vegetables, cover and simmer over medium heat for 10 minutes, stirring occasionally. Add hot broth, tomatoes, pepper, and bay leaves. Cover and simmer over medium heat for 35 minutes, stirring occasionally. Stir in hominy. Set cover slightly ajar, and simmer over medium-high heat for 10 minutes. Remove bay leaves and add chopped parsley. Serve at once with thick slices of toasted French bread.

CARLO GATTI: THE SWISS INVENTOR OF THE ICE CREAM CONE

Carlo Gatti, whose name is inextricably linked with the history of ice cream, was the first to make ice cream available to ordinary people, and he was also the inventor of the *Glace-Cornet*, the waffle ice cream cone.

Carlo Gatti was born in 1817 in Marogno in the Val Blenio as the eldest of six children. At the age of 13, he left his home and traveled on foot to Paris, where members of his family already lived. Carlo was a poor student, and everything that led to his success in his later professional life, he learned on the street. At first, he tried his hand at all sorts of activities, but nothing seemed to really work out for him. For a time, he earned his living by selling roasted chestnuts. His relatives were relieved when he decided to move to London and seek his fortune there in 1847.

In London, he moved to Holborn, where many Italian and Ticinese immigrants lived at that time, also including Gatti's relatives. At first, he opened his own stall and sold sugared waffles, and roasted chestnuts in the winter. Two years later, together with Batista Bolla, another Ticinese, he founded a business initially manufacturing and selling ice cream. Much has been written and speculated about that ice cream and about Gatti's first retail shop. However, there is evidence it was in that shop that ice cream was offered to the public at large for the first time. Up to that point, ice cream had been very expensive and had been served only at the exclusive tables of the wealthy. Utilizing his previous experience as a waffle seller for his new area of business, Gatti developed the waffle cone, which is used as a holder for scoops of ice cream and soft ice cream to this day. That is why Carlo Gatti is justifiably revered as the father of the ice cream cone.

In the 1850s, ice cream production was a big challenge. Rich households occasionally had cooling cellars they filled with ice blocks in the winter which could later be used for refrigeration until the summer. Ice cream was also manufactured from those blocks. However, the method was not suitable for industrial production. For that reason, Gatti began to import large quantities of ice from Norway for his business. The ice blocks were cut with saws in mountain lakes in southern Norway, transported to the ports on special railroad cars, and loaded onto big sailing ships there. Via the Thames River, the ships arrived at Battlebridge Basin near King's Cross, where Gatti had his ice warehouse operation.

But the ice king did not restrict himself to manufacturing and sales. Soon he had several horse-drawn wagons which he used to deliver ice to private households and restaurants. Gatti became London's largest ice importer.

In 1857, inspired by the Parisian way of life, Carlo Gatti opened a music hall, which became famous under the name Gatti's. Five years later, he sold the music hall to South Eastern Railway, and Charing Cross railway station was built on the site. Gatti invested the proceeds he obtained in a new music hall and a restaurant. From 1871 on, he spent most of his time in Switzerland again, and he handed over his businesses to relatives.

Carlo Gatti is remembered not only as the inventor of the waffle cone and of ice cream for the masses, but also as a creative mind and an innovator. He instinctively recognized the economic potential in many new things and was able to transform his knowledge into a successful business model. He brought ice cream and the waffle together, improved cold storage methods, and combined his attractive product with musical entertainment and recreational activity.

Today Gatti's former ice warehouse houses the London Canal Museum, which recalls the ice wells and the beginnings of the ice and ice cream business. Of course, there were early forms of ice cream long before that time. Even in antiquity, the Persians are said to have mixed snow with fruit. Historical records from the Tang Dynasty (618–907) tell of a great number of icemen at the court of the Chinese emperor. Furthermore there are unreliable reports that, in addition to pasta, Marco Polo is also supposed to have brought ice cream from China to Europe. Caterina de' Medici is also supposed to have earned credit for ice cream. In the 1660s, the first sorbets appeared in Italy, Spain, and France. An ice cream with sweetened milk is supposed to have been successfully produced for the first time in 1664. There are many recipes and historical records from the following decades that recall production methods such as that for ice cream. Cold creamy desserts made from egg white, sugar, and fruit have been served since the mid-eighteenth century. Although ice cream continued to be a luxury product in the nineteenth century, it gradually became available to more people. Ice cream in cones was a genuine innovation. Ice cream was often licked from shallow glasses; the glasses were rinsed at ice cream stands and reused, which was unhygienic. In England, such glasses were called a "penny lick" and contained ice cream for a penny. Wrapped in waxed paper, ice cream in London was called "hokey pokey," which probably comes from the Italian expression *Ecce un poco* ("Here is a little").

The following rare ice cream desserts tell stories about Swiss people and Switzerland. They are served from an ice cream cart on special occasions at the Embassy of Switzerland in Washington.

GRAPE AND PORT ICE CREAM (RITZ HOTELS)

Makes 1 pint

ICE CREAM BASE

1 cup heavy cream
1 cup whole milk
4 egg yolks

⅓ cup sugar

Combine heavy cream and milk in a saucepan and bring it to a simmer, making sure it does not boil over.

Meanwhile, whisk the egg yolks and sugar in a bowl until the mixture has thickened and the color has turned pale.

Slowly pour a third of the hot cream into the yolk mixture, whisking constantly to prevent the yolks from curdling, then add the rest of the hot cream and whisk to combine.

Return the egg and cream mixture to the saucepan and put it back on the burner on medium heat. Whisk the mixture constantly until it thickens and coats the back of a spoon.

Pass the cream through a sieve into a bowl and refrigerate it for at least 4 hours or overnight.

GRAPE AND PORT ICE CREAM

1 ice cream base recipe
3 cups of 100% pure organic grape juice
½ cup Ruby Port wine
2 tablespoons sugar
1 star anise
1 cinnamon stick

Add the grape juice, port wine, sugar, star anise and cinnamon stick to a saucepan and bring it to a simmer and cook until liquid has reduced to 1 cup. Strain the grape mixture into a bowl and let it cool completely.

Add the grape mixture to the ice cream base and whisk to combine. Refrigerate for at least 4 hours. Pour the chilled mixture into an ice cream machine bowl and freeze according to the manufacturer's instructions.

Transfer to a container and place in the freezer until ready to use.

ALMOND CRUNCH ICE CREAM (RITZ HOTEL)

Makes 1 pint

FOR THE CARAMELIZED ALMOND CRUNCH

> *½ cup sliced almonds*
> *2 tablespoons sugar*
> *Pinch of fine sea salt*

FOR THE ICE CREAM

> *1 cup sliced almonds, toasted*
> *1 cup heavy cream*
> *1 cup milk*
> *½ cup sugar*
> *6 egg yolks*
> *¼ teaspoon fine sea salt*
> *¼ teaspoon bitter almond extract*

TO MAKE THE CARAMELIZED ALMOND CRUNCH

Add the sliced almonds with the sugar and salt to a pan and cook on medium heat until golden and caramelized, about 10 minutes. Transfer to a plate and reserve.

TO MAKE THE ICE CREAM

Put the heavy cream, milk and sliced almonds into a saucepan and bring it to a simmer. Let it simmer for about 10 minutes, making sure it does not boil over. Take the pan from the heat and let it sit aside for an hour.

Whisk the egg yolks and sugar until thick and pale.

Bring the cream and almond mixture back to a simmer and then very slowly pour a third of it into the yolk mixture, whisking constantly, then add the rest of the cream and whisk to combine. Pour all of the cream back into the saucepan and put on the burner on medium heat and whisk constantly until it thickens and coats the back of a spoon.

Pass the mixture through a sieve into a bowl and add the salt. Place the mixture in the refrigerator for at least 4 hours.

Take the mixture from the refrigerator and add the bitter almond extract. Pour the mixture into an ice cream machine bowl and freeze it according to the manufacturer's instructions.

Break the almond crunch into small pieces and add to the ice cream 2 minutes before the ice cream has finished churning.

Transfer to a container and place in the freezer until ready to use.

CHERRY ICE CREAM (RITZ HOTELS)

Makes 1 pint

> *1 ice cream base recipe (see above)*
> *2 cups of sweet black cherries (fresh or frozen), pitted*
> *⅓ cup kirsch*
> *4 tablespoons sugar*
> *1 teaspoon pure vanilla extract*

Marinate the cherries and kirsch with sugar in a saucepan for 1 hour. Put the pan on the burner on medium heat and cook for 10 minutes. Take the pan off the heat and let cool completely. Blend the cherries and kirsch in a food processor until smooth. Add the cherry kirsch mixture to the ice cream base and whisk to combine. Refrigerate for at least 4 hours. *Pour the mixture into an ice cream machine bowl and freeze according to manufacturer's instructions.*

Transfer to a container and place in the freezer until ready to use.

SWISS DARK CHOCOLATE ICE CREAM (DELMONICO'S)

Makes 1 pint

> 1 cup milk
> 1 cup heavy cream
> 1 vanilla bean
> ½ cup Dutch cocoa powder
> 1 egg
> 1 egg yolk
> 1 teaspoon pure vanilla extract
> 6 oz. dark Swiss chocolate (73%)

Add the milk and cream to a saucepan. Split the vanilla bean in half with a thin blade knife and scrape out the seeds. Add both seeds and vanilla shell to cream and bring it to a simmer.

Simmer for 10 minutes, making sure it does not boil over. Set aside.

Whisk the egg, egg yolk, sugar and cocoa powder with a hand mixer until creamy. Strain a third of the hot cream into the egg mixture and whisk to combine.

Strain the remaining cream into a clean pot and bring to a simmer. Add the chocolate to the hot cream in the pot and stir until melted. Slowly add the hot chocolate cream mixture into the egg mixture, whisking constantly until well blended. Return the entire mixture to the saucepan and cook on medium heat until chocolate cream has thickened, resembling a pudding. Pass the chocolate mixture through a sieve into a bowl and chill for at least 4 hours. Add the vanilla extract and whisk to combine. Pour the mixture into an ice cream machine bowl and freeze according to manufacturer's instructions.

Transfer to a container and place in the freezer until ready to use.

COFFEE ICE CREAM (SWISS CONFECTIONERS')

In the old days, Swiss confectioners were famous and worked throughout Europe. When they were still children, they learned their craft at home or from relatives; then they left home at a young age. Many Swiss confectioners came from the poor mountain regions in Grisons, in eastern Switzerland. Swiss confectioners did more than make and sell pastry; they ran coffee shops, made liquor and ice cream as well. This recipe is from Perini's once famous book *Schweizerzuckerbäcker* (Swiss Confectioners).

Makes 1 pint

> *1½ cups cream*
> *1½ cups milk*
> *⅓ cup sugar*
> *4 egg yolks*
> *¼ cup roasted whole coffee beans*
> *¼ cup very strong espresso*

Place cream, milk, sugar and coffee beans into a saucepan and bring to a simmer and let it simmer for about 5 minutes. Turn off the heat and let steep until completely cold.

Pour the mixture into a blender and blend for a few seconds until the coffee beans are broken, but not ground. Pass the liquid through a fine sieve back into the saucepan. Add the espresso and bring the liquid back to a simmer.

Whisk the egg yolks until pale and thick and add a third of the hot cream, whisking constantly, then add the rest of the hot cream and stir to combine.

Pour the cream and egg mixture back into the saucepan and cook on medium heat until the cream has thickened and coats the back of a spoon. Strain the mixture into a bowl and refrigerate for at least 4 hours.

Pour the cooled mixture into an ice cream machine bowl and proceed according to manufacturer's instructions.

Transfer to a container and place in the freezer until ready to use.

CHESTNUT AND CHOCOLATE SHAVES ICE CREAM (OSCAR OF THE WALDORF)

Makes 1 pint

> *1 ice cream base recipe (see above)*
> *12 oz. chestnut purée*
> *1 teaspoon pure vanilla extract*
> *½ cup small chocolate shaves or curls*

Blend the chestnut purée with half of the ice cream base in a food processor. Pour the mixture into the other half of the ice cream base and add the vanilla extract and whisk until well combined. Refrigerate for at least 4 hours.

Pour the cooled mixture into an ice cream machine bowl and proceed according to manufacturer's instructions.

Add the chocolate shaves 2 minutes before the churning process is finished.

Transfer to a container and place in the freezer until ready to use.

ORANGE ICE CREAM
(OSCAR OF THE WALDORF)

Makes 1 pint

> 1 ice cream base recipe
> 2 cups fresh orange juice
> 1½ tablespoons orange liqueur
> 2 tablespoons sugar
> 1 vanilla bean, split in half and seeded
> 1 cinnamon stick
> 1 star anise
> Zest of half orange (long strips)
> 2 oz. butter

Add the orange juice, orange liqueur, sugar, vanilla, cinnamon, star anise and orange zest to a saucepan and stir to combine.

Put the pan on a burner and, on medium heat, reduce the liquid to 1 cup. Strain the reduction into a bowl and add the butter and stir until melted and incorporated into the reduction. Let it cool to room temperature.

Add the orange and butter reduction to the ice cream base and whisk to combine. Refrigerate for at least 4 hours.

Pour the cooled mixture into an ice cream machine bowl and proceed according to manufacturer's instructions.

Transfer to a container and place in the freezer until ready to use.

If desired, candied orange peel can be added to the ice cream 2 minutes before the churning process is finished.

CARAMEL SWIRL ICE CREAM
(OSCAR OF THE WALDORF)

Makes 1 pint

> *4 tablespoons butter (1/2 stick)*
> *½ cup brown sugar*
> *¼ teaspoon fine sea salt*
> *4 egg yolks*
> *½ teaspoon pure vanilla extract*
> *1½ cups heavy cream*
> *1 cup milk*
> *1 cup caramel sauce (recipe follows)*

Add the butter to a saucepan on medium heat and cook it stirring occasionally until the butter turns a deep golden color and you see dark flecks. Take the pan off the heat and add the brown sugar and stir to combine. Put the pan back on the stove on medium heat and cook the butter and sugar mixture until the sugar is melted. Add a ½ cup of cream and stir until all is combined and cook for another 2 minutes.

Add the remaining cream, milk and salt to the mixture and stir to combine and bring it to a simmer.

In a bowl, whisk the egg yolks until they turn pale.

Slowly pour a third of the hot cream mixture into the yolks, stirring constantly, then pour the egg mixture back into the saucepan and mix with the rest of the cream. Cook the egg mixture on medium heat until it thickens and coats the back of a spoon. Strain the custard through a fine sieve into a bowl and refrigerate for at least 4 hours.

Pour the cooled mixture into an ice cream machine bowl and proceed according to manufacturer's instructions.

One minute before the churning process is finished, slowly pour in the caramel sauce in a thin stream and let it swirl in the ice cream. Turn the machine off as soon as all the caramel has been poured in.

Transfer to a container and place in the freezer until ready to use.

CARAMEL

> 1 cup sugar
> ¼ cup water
> ½ cup cream
> 2 oz. butter
> 1 teaspoon fine sea salt

Combine sugar and water in a saucepan and cook it on low heat until the sugar has dissolved, then increase the temperature to high and bring it to a boil and cook the sugar until it starts to turn an amber color. Take the pan from the heat and swirl the pan around to release the sugar crystals that formed around the pan. The sugar will continue cooking, turning darker even when removed from the heat. Add the cream to the caramel and stir until all is combined. Put the pan back on the burner and cook for another minute. Remove from heat and add the butter and salt and whisk to combine. Pour the caramel into a bowl and let it cool completely. Store the caramel in a glass jar with a lid in the refrigerator.

APPLE SORBET (JOSEPH FAVRE)

Makes 1 pint

> 5 large Granny Smith apples
> ½ cup sugar
> 2 tablespoons fresh lemon juice

Peel, core and roughly chop the apples.

Add the apples, sugar and lemon juice to a saucepan and cook on medium heat until the apples are soft. Remove the pan from the heat and let it cool completely.

Add the apples and juice from the pan to a blender and blend until very smooth like applesauce. Transfer the applesauce to a bowl and refrigerate for at least 4 hours.

Pour the cooled mixture into an ice cream machine bowl and proceed according to manufacturer's instructions.

Transfer to a container and place in the freezer until ready to use.

MELON SORBET (JOSEPH FAVRE)

Makes 1 pint

> *1 small ripe cantaloupe*
> *½ cup sugar*
> *1 vanilla bean*
> *1 lemon, zested and juiced*

Peel and seed the cantaloupe and cut into small chunks.

Place the cantaloupe into a saucepan and add sugar. Split and scrape the vanilla bean and add to the pan. Add the zest and juice of 1 lemon. Stir everything together and cook until the melon is soft and the sugar has dissolved and thickened a little, about 10 or 15 minutes. Take the pan off the heat and let it cool completely.

Remove the vanilla bean from the pan and discard it. Add the remaining contents in the pan to a blender and blend until very smooth. Strain the liquid through a fine sieve into a bowl and refrigerate for at least 4 hours.

Pour the cooled mixture into an ice cream machine bowl and proceed according to manufacturer's instructions.

Transfer to a container and place in the freezer until ready to use.

CHEF HALLER'S PEACH ICE CREAM

Makes 1 pint

> *1 ice cream base recipe*
> *6 very ripe peaches*
> *½ cup sugar*
> *1 tablespoon pure vanilla extract*

Blanch the peaches in boiling water for 20 seconds, then place them in ice water and immediately peel them. Remove the pit and cut them into small dices. Place the peaches in a bowl with sugar and vanilla extract and let them sit for about 1 hour until the sugar has dissolved. Blend half of the peaches in a food processor until smooth. Reserve the other half. Add the pureed peach to the ice cream base and whisk to combine and refrigerate for at least 4 hours. Pour the mixture into an ice cream machine bowl and freeze according to manufacturer's instructions. Add the reserved chopped peaches into the ice cream 2 minutes before the churning process is finished.

Transfer to a container and place in the freezer until ready to use.

SWISS DESSERTS AND
THE STORIES BEHIND THEM

Before cheese and chocolate became world famous as Swiss specialties, Swiss confectioners spread the country's culinary reputation throughout Europe. In the mountainous region, where there was no natural resource exploitation and agriculture was limited, there was not always enough food for the population. Many young men hoped to find a way out of extreme poverty by becoming mercenaries, others went abroad to seek their fortunes as confectioners. When they were still children, they learned their trade at home from their parents or from their relatives, and they left home as adolescents. Many of them came from the valleys of the Canton of Graubünden.

Swiss confectioners who immigrated to other countries can be traced as far back as the fifteenth century. The Republic of Venice was the most promising destination at first. The Swiss sold their sweets in the alleyways of the city. But they also served coffee, spirits and beverages of all kinds. In 1704, 95 of Venice's 104 confectioner's shops were under the ownership of *Bündner*, that is, people originally from Graubünden. They ran their businesses themselves for the most part, but sometimes they leased them to others. The vast majority of the sellers of spirits came from Graubünden, too.

After a trade dispute between the Republic of Venice and Graubünden, all the Swiss confectioners were driven out of Venice in 1766. For those affected by it, the prohibition from practicing their trade was a dramatic and decisive point in their lives; for the Swiss confectioner's trade, however, it was a stroke of luck since Swiss confectioners soon began to settle throughout Europe. The height of the confectioner's trade was the period between the French Revolution and the middle of the nineteenth century. The abolishment of compulsory guild membership occurred in many countries at that time, making market entry easier for foreigners. In the mid-nineteenth century, almost 10,000 confectioners from Graubünden worked in over a thousand villages and towns in Europe. While Italy remained an important center, Swiss confectioners also settled in Germany, Scandinavia, and Eastern Europe, from Warsaw to Saint Petersburg. Following the old business model, many emigrants also founded cafés in addition to confectioner's shops. The famous establishments include Café Josty in Berlin and Café Chinois in Saint Petersburg. The legendary Delmonico's in New York was also originally a confectioner's shop that sold coffee.

The following recipes come from different eras and recall significant figures and events in Swiss history.

WILHELM TELL CAKE

The *Wilhelm Tell Cake* recalls the legendary Swiss national hero. The Tell saga's central theme, the murder of the tyrant, did not please everybody. Dramas and operas about Wilhelm Tell were prohibited many times, including in Germany during the Nazi period. The Wilhelm Tell Cake, however, has never been prohibited.

> *¾ cup sugar*
> *6 egg yolks*
> *1 lemon, grated zest & juice*
> *6 egg whites*
> *1 pinch of salt*
> *1⅔ cups flour, sifted*
> *4 large red apples*
> *6 tablespoons apricot jam*

Preheat the oven to 350° F and grease a 15'' x 14'' baking pan.

Beat the sugar and egg yolk until light and foamy, and then stir in lemon zest.

Beat the egg whites with a pinch of salt until stiff and set aside.
Peel half of the apples, remove core and grate. Add a bit of lemon juice and set aside.

Remove the core from the remaining apples and cut them into six slices each. Dip them into lemon juice and set aside.

Now carefully add the flour to the egg yolk mixture and mix the flour, constantly alternating the grated apples with the egg whites.

Fill the mixture into a prepared pan, and add the apple slices as a top layer (do not press down). Bake for about 25 minutes and let the cake cool completely.

Melt the apricot jam and brush onto cake. Cut into squares before serving.

Torta Elvezia

Helvetia is the personification of Switzerland as a nation. Usually Helvetia is represented as a woman with a shield, spear and a laurel wreath, sometimes with a mountain ridge in the background. Helvetia's face looks very similar to that of the American Lady Liberty; they could be sisters. Both figures were inspired by sculptures from the time of the Roman Republic. Swiss coins and stamps depict HELVETIA, which is far easier than using the names for Switzerland in the four national languages. *Torta Elvezia* is a popular cake in Ticino, the Italian-speaking southern part of Switzerland. This recipe is by Paola Chizzini.

Makes one 11'' cake

CAKE LAYERS

7 egg whites
1½ cups confectioners' sugar
⅔ cup hazelnuts, finely ground
2 cups almonds, finely ground
½ cup granulated sugar
1 pinch of salt

ZABAIONE

4 egg yolks
4 tablespoons white wine
4 tablespoons Marsala
8 tablespoons granulated sugar

BUTTERCREAM

1 cup butter, room temperature
1½ cups confectioners' sugar

ASSEMBLY

1 cup chocolate shaves
¾ cup hazelnuts, chopped

Preheat the oven to 350° F. Draw three 11'' circles on three sheets of parchment paper. Line three baking trays with the papers and set aside.

Mix hazelnuts, almonds and granulated sugar in a bowl and set aside. Beat egg whites with salt until stiff peaks form. Stir in confectioners' sugar until the mixture starts to look shiny. Now carefully fold the nuts into the egg whites. Fill the mixture into a piping bag with a round opening. Now pipe the mixture onto the three prepared baking sheets, always starting from the outside and moving in spirals toward the middle, until the circle is full with mixture. Bake for approximately 20 minutes and let the layers cool on a rack.

Meanwhile prepare the Zabaione: beat the egg yolks and granulated sugar with a standing mixture for five minutes. Transfer the bowl onto a pot of boiling water, add white wine and Marsala; stir continuously until mixture starts to thicken and looks creamy. Remove the bowl from the water bath, pour the cream into a container, let it cool and refrigerate until further use.

For the buttercream, mix butter with a standing mixture for two minutes. Gradually add confectioners' sugar until a smooth frosting has formed.

Now assemble the cake: spread about a third of buttercream onto one cake layer and top with half of the Zabaione cream. Sprinkle with chocolate shaves before setting the second layer on top and repeating the same process. Cover with the third cake layer and spread the remaining butter cream on around the sides of the cake only. Press hazelnuts and chocolate shaves on the sides so the frosting is not visible anymore. Refrigerate the cake and sprinkle with powdered sugar before serving. The cake tastes best when eaten fresh.

MATTERHORN MACAROONS

The Matterhorn is the most photographed tourist attraction in Switzerland and the most photographed mountain in the world. On July 14, 1865, the famous British alpinist Edward Whymper succeeded in a dramatic race in being the first to reach the peak of the Matterhorn. Since then, many people have climbed the mountain, including President Theodore Roosevelt during his honeymoon. In 1979, the Matterhorn Bobsleds opened at Disneyland in Anaheim, California, and they are still roaring today on the mountain modeled after the Matterhorn. The much smaller Matterhorn Macaroons are also modeled after the iconic mountain.

Makes approximately 15-20 pieces

>*4 cups grated coconut*
>*1⅓ cups condensed milk, sweetened*
>*1 egg white*
>*¼ teaspoon vanilla extract*
>*1 pinch of salt*
>*White chocolate*
>*Powdered sugar for garnishing*

Preheat the oven to 300° F and line a baking sheet with parchment paper.

Mix coconut flakes, condensed milk, salt and vanilla extract in a bowl. Beat the egg white until stiff and gently fold into the coconut mixture. With your hands, form small Matterhorn Macaroons (about 1-2 tablespoon of mixture each) and put them on the baking tray.

Bake the Matterhorns for 25 to 30 minutes until they are golden brown. Let them cool on a rack.

Melt the white chocolate in the microwave, then pour it over the Matterhorns. After the chocolate has set, sprinkle powdered sugar over the top.

TOBLERONE MOUSSE

The Swiss were pioneers in making chocolate and are still the people with the highest per-capita consumption of chocolate. The famous Toblerone was invented by Theodor Tobler in the city of Bern in 1908. When Theodor Tobler applied for a patent for Toblerone, Albert Einstein was working as a technical expert at the Federal Patent Office in Bern. No one knows whether Einstein processed the application. Toblerone is sometimes misspelled as Tobler One. The name

Toblerone is a play on words linking the inventor's name Tobler with Torrone, the Italian word for honey-almond-nougat mix.

Serves 4-5

> *5½ oz. (2 bars) Toblerone of any kind, depending on preference*
> *Hot water*
> *1 egg*
> *1 tablespoon confectioners' sugar*
> *⅔ cup heavy cream*
> *½ cup white chocolate couverture*

Whip the cream until stiff, set aside. Break 1½ Toblerone bars into pieces and put them in a wide bowl. Pour boiling water over it and wait until chocolate is melted (use a knife or toothpick to test). Remove the water and stir the chocolate until smooth.

Beat egg and confectioners' sugar in a bowl for about 4 minutes (color should turn very light). Stir in the melted chocolate and fold in the whipped cream. Divide into small pots before cooling or cool in one large bowl. Refrigerate for at least three hours.

Melt the white couverture and pour it into a piping bag and cut a very small edge off. With quick movements, pipe random grids onto the mousse for decoration. Crumble some of the leftover Toblerone on top and serve.

HIRSEBREI: SWEET MILLET GRUEL
AS IN THE MIDDLE AGES

Millet was one of the most important nutrients in the Middle Ages. No other grain is so rich in minerals, albumen, and amino acids. Sweetened with sugar or honey, it makes a lovely dessert. A long time ago, the citizens of Zurich claimed that they were so quick in reinforcing their allies in Strasbourg that in case of a siege they could reach them with a millet gruel that was still warm. In 1456, they tested it out and arrived at their destination with food that was still hot. Every ten years, that historic journey is reenacted. However, the river locks, power plants and other obstacles in the water make it a much longer journey than in the Middle Ages.

Serves 4-6

> *1 cup millet*
> *3 cups milk*
> *1½–2½ tablespoons honey*
> *⅔ cup raisins*
> *⅓ cup hazelnuts, chopped*
> *⅓ cup walnuts, chopped*
> *⅓ cup dried fruit*

Bring the milk to a boil and add millet. Cook over low heat, stirring from time to time for about 45 minutes until the grains have softened completely. If necessary, add more milk while cooking. At the end, add honey to taste, serve in small bowls and top with raisins, nuts and dried fruit. Best when served hot and fresh, but it can also be enjoyed cold.

CHERRY PIE (MAESTRO MARTINO)

Makes one 11'' pie

CRUST

> *2½ cups flour*
> *1 cup butter*
> *¼ cup sugar*
> *Grated zest of 1 lemon*
> *¼–½ cup ice water*

FILLING

> ⅔ lb. ricotta
> 2 eggs
> 1 cup sugar
> 1 teaspoon cinnamon
> 1 teaspoon ginger
> ⅔ lb. sour cherries, canned

For the crust, combine flour, butter, sugar, egg yolks, and lemon zest. Work dough vigorously, cover, let set in cool place for 30 minutes.

Preheat oven to 350° F. Grease a pie tin and set aside. Pass the ricotta through a sieve, combine with eggs, sugar, cinnamon, ginger, rose water, and cherries.

Divide the dough into two pieces and roll it out slightly bigger than the pie tin. Use one sheet of dough to line pie tin. Add the filling and spread evenly. Use remaining dough to make lattice top. Bake for 45 minutes and let cool before serving.

SCHWEIZER KRÖPFLI
(SWISS CONFECTIONERS)

Schweizer Kröpfli is a recipe from Perini's famous *Cookbook for Swiss Confectioners.*

Makes 50-60 pieces

SHORTBREAD CRUST

> 3¾ cups flour
> 2 tablespoons brandy
> 1 lemon, zested
> 2 eggs
> 9 oz. butter

9 oz. sugar

ASSEMBLY

2 eggs
¾ cup apricot, quince or raspberry jam

SHORTBREAD

Mix butter, sugar, lemon zest and eggs for about 4 minutes. Sift the flour onto the mixture; slowly incorporate just until combined. Wrap the dough into foil and refrigerate for one hour.

Assembly:

Preheat the oven to 390° F and line several baking sheets with parchment paper. Separate the two remaining eggs and mix the egg yolk with two teaspoons of milk. Roll the dough out, about two-tenths of an inch thick. If the dough is too sticky, sprinkle it lightly with flour. With a cookie cutter, cut out 2'' circles and place them on the prepared baking sheets. Heat the jam until lukewarm, place one teaspoon of jam in the middle of each circle and brush the sides with egg white. Fold each cake from three sides and lightly press them together in the middle. Brush the cakes with egg yolk-milk mixture, refrigerate for one hour before baking the cakes for 10 minutes. Let them cool on a rack before serving.

BABA AU RHUM (DELMONICO'S)

Makes 10 Babas

BABA PASTE

1⅔ cups flour
½ stick butter
2 tablespoons granulated sugar

1 pinch of salt
2 eggs
1 tablespoons candied oranges, diced
2 tablespoons raisins
1 tablespoons dried currants
2-3 tablespoons warm milk

SYRUP

10 tablespoons water
¾ cup granulated sugar
7 tablespoons orange juice
9 tablespoons rum
1 vanilla bean

BABA PASTE

Mix flour, yeast, sugar and salt in a large bowl. Melt the butter and add it to the flour mixture together with the eggs and 2 tablespoons of milk. Mix and knead to smooth dough. Incorporate the candied oranges, raisins and dried currants. If the paste is too dry, carefully add more milk (only little by little). Put the paste back into the bowl, cover with a damp towel and let it rise for about an hour in a warm place.

SYRUP

Boil water and granulated sugar for about five minutes, stirring occasionally. Scrape the vanilla bean and add the vanilla pulp, orange juice and rum to the sugar syrup. Cook for another three minutes and pour into another container to cool.

Assembly:

Preheat the oven to 350° F. Grease ten Baba molds, divide the paste among them and let them rise for another 20 minutes in a warm place. Bake for approximately ten minutes, leave to cool for about ten minutes and then poke various holes with a toothpick into each cake. Pour the syrup over the cakes until you have used up all of it. The paste soaks up the entire liquid; however, do not add all the syrup at once, but in 10-20 minute intervals. Once all the syrup is used up, let the Babas set for 5-6 hours, best overnight. Optionally garnish with heavy whipped cream and rum before serving.

SWISS MACAROONS
(OSCAR OF THE WALDORF)

Makes about 60 pieces

 2½ cups blanched almond flour
 1¾ cups granulated sugar
 3 egg whites
 ¼ cup almonds, sliced

Preheat the oven to 300° F and line two baking trays with parchment paper. Beat the egg whites until stiff and set aside. Mix granulated sugar and almond flour and then fold in the egg whites. Fill the mixture into a piping bag with a large star tip and pipe 1'' puffs onto the prepared baking trays. Top each macaroon with 1-2 almond slices. Bake for about 15 minutes, until the edges start to turn golden and leave to cool on the tray.

BERNER LECKERLI
(HENRY HALLER)

The recipe for *Berner Leckerli* is from Henry Haller's *The White House Family Cookbook.*

Makes 30

LECKERLI BASE

> *1 cup coarsely ground almonds*
> *1 cup coarsely ground hazelnuts*
> *2 cups granulated sugar*
> *½ cup flour*
> *2 teaspoons cinnamon*
> *½ cup finely grated orange peel*
> *1 tablespoons honey*
> *5-6 egg whites*

KIRSCH GLAZE

> *1½ cups confectioners' sugar*
> *½ cup water*
> *1 teaspoons kirsch*

BASE

In a large bowl, combine the nuts, sugar, flour, and cinnamon. Stir in orange peel and honey. Beat the egg whites until stiff and fold into mixture, which should be very moist. If it is not, add more egg whites. Press the dough into a square, cover tightly with plastic wrap, refrigerate for at least six hours.

Preheat oven to 350° F. Line one baking sheet with parchment paper. Spread the dough onto the baking sheet, about ½ inch thick. Bake for 5-6 minutes, cool for five minutes and cut into 1'' x 2'' rectangles before frosting.

GLAZE

For the glaze: mix water, sugar and kirsch and brush onto cut cookies. Let the Leckerli cool and set completely.

COCKTAILS SERVED
AT THE SWISS RESIDENCE
IN WASHINGTON

Mixed drinks can be traced back to prehistoric times. But they are the most authentic contribution of the United States to culinary history. Bars and alcoholic drinks played an important role in the conquest of the vast country and in the evolution of modern urban life. Mixed drinks are created for special occasions; many are named after famous people, places or memorable events, making them an abundant source of cultural history as well.

The seventeen mixed drinks in this booklet recall remarkable topics related to Switzerland, but they are not traditional Swiss drinks. They are served on special occasions at the Swiss Residence in Washington, D.C.

THE ASTORIA

Add 1 oz. of gin and 2 oz. of Noilly Prat vermouth and 2 dashes of orange bitters to a shaker and shake until chilled. Strain into a martini glass and serve immediately.

The Astoria cocktail was created by Oscar of the Waldorf and published in the book *100 Famous Cocktails* in 1934.

CHARLIE CHAPLIN

Add 0.6 oz. of apricot brandy, 0.6 oz. of sloe gin and the juice of half a lemon to a shaker. Add ice to the shaker and shake until chilled. Strain into a martini glass and serve immediately with a lemon twist as garnish.

Charles Spencer "Charlie" Chaplin (1889–1977) was an English comic actor, filmmaker, and composer who became famous during the silent film era. His career spanned more than 75 years, from his childhood in the Victorian era until a year before his death. He is considered one of the most important figures in the history of the film industry. In 1953, Charlie Chaplin settled in Corsier-sur-Vevey on the banks of Lake Geneva, in Switzerland, where he is also buried. The *Chaplin's World* museum opened on his former estate, Manoir le Ban, in 2016.

The *Charlie Chaplin* is quite a common short drink. The recipe was published in *The Old Waldorf-Astoria Bar Book* in 1935.

DELMONICO

Add 0.6 oz. of cognac, 0.6 oz. of gin, 0.6 oz. of dry vermouth, 0.6 oz. of vermouth rosso and one dash of Angostura bitters to a shaker. Add ice to the shaker and shake until chilled. Strain into a short glass and serve immediately with an orange peel as garnish.

The *Delmonico cocktail* is a short drink created at Delmonico's bar in New York. The recipe was published in *The Old Waldorf-Astoria Bar Book* in 1935.

FIFTY SEVEN CHEVY

Add 1 oz. of Southern Comfort, 1 oz. of whiskey, 1 oz. of Amaretto and one dash of grenadine to a shaker. Add ice to the shaker and shake until chilled. Strain into a highball glass filled with ice and top up with equal parts of orange and pineapple juice.

Born in 1878 in the Swiss city La Chaux-de-Fonds, Louis Chevrolet moved in 1901 to the United States, where he soon became idolized as a racing car driver and a skilled car builder. In 1911, he founded the Chevrolet Motor Company of Michigan, laying the foundations for the legendary car brand that soon conquered the streets with the famous Chevy. The Chevrolet logo resembles the Swiss cross. The 1957 Chevrolet, developed long after Chevrolet's time, is a car model frequently found in toys, graphics, music, movies, and television. The seductive *Fifty Seven Chevy* cocktail captures the car's glamour.

GOLDEN GATE 75

Add 1 oz. of Campari, 1 oz. of blood orange juice, 0.5 oz. of simple syrup and 1 dash of orange bitters to a shaker. Add ice to the shaker and shake until chilled. To remove any pulp, strain well into a champagne glass and top with chilled sparkling wine. Serve immediately with orange zest as garnish.

This cocktail commemorated the Golden Gate Bridge's 75th anniversary in 2012. The Swiss-American engineer Othmar Ammann (1879–1965) played an important role in the construction of the Golden Gate Bridge. Ammann, a graduate of the Swiss Federal Institute of Technology in Zurich, designed and directed many important infrastructure projects in the United States, including the George Washington Bridge and the Lincoln Tunnel in New York.

The *Golden Gate 75* is a cocktail similar to the well-known cocktail *French 75*. By replacing gin and lemon with Campari and blood orange juice, the drink takes on the color of the iconic bridge in San Francisco. The drink was created by the journalist Camper English.

GOTTHARD COCKTAIL

Add 1 oz. of rum, 0.5 oz. of Amaro Braulio, 0.5 oz. of Blue Curaçao, 0.5 oz. of Kirsch, 0.25 oz. of lemon juice and 0.25 oz. of simple syrup to a shaker. Add ice to the shaker and shake until chilled. Strain into a short glass. Serve immediately with an edible flower as garnish.

The Saint-Gotthard Massif is a unique mountain range in the Swiss Alps that has played an important role since time immemorial. It is an important passage from the Mediterranean to Northern Europe, and it is the separation line between the German and Italian languages. In 1882, the Gotthard Railway Tunnel was opened, and in 2016, the Gotthard Base Tunnel became the world's longest tunnel. The event was commemorated all over the world, including at the annual Soirée Suisse at the Embassy of Switzerland in Washington, D.C., in September 2016.

The *Gotthard Cocktail* is a creation of the Embassy of Switzerland, inspired by Luisito Cericetti's Gotthard Special. It uses Amaro Braulio instead of the difficult-to-find Weisflog Bitter.

KRONENHALLE ROYAL

Add 0.3 oz. of Grand Marnier Rouge, 0.3 oz. of Crème de cassis and one dash of Angostura bitters to a shaker. Add ice to the shaker and shake until chilled. Strain into a regular glass and top with 4 oz. of chilled champagne. Serve immediately with a lemon twist or an orange spiral as garnish.

The Kronenhalle is a flagship restaurant in Zurich, Switzerland's largest city and economic powerhouse. The Kronenhalle was the meeting point of actors, artists, writers, and celebrities such as James Joyce, Pablo Picasso, Oskar Kokoschka, Joan Mirò, Alberto Giacometti, Vladimir Horowitz, Lauren Bacall, Rudolf Nureyev, Andy Warhol, Yves Saint Laurent, and Winston Churchill. Among its most regular guests were Swiss writers and playwrights Friedrich Dürrenmatt and Max Frisch.

The *Kronenhalle Royal* is an elegant long drink named after the place where the well-known bartender Paul Nüesch prepared mixed drinks for his illustrious guests.

MAZAGRAN À LA GÉNÉRAL DUFOUR

Fill a short glass with ice and pour one freshly brewed espresso. Add 1 oz. of Kirsch and stir with a spoon.

Guillaume-Henri Dufour (1787–1875) was a Swiss army officer, engineer, and topographer. He served under Napoleon and commanded the Federal Army against the Sonderbund forces in 1847. Dufour designed the Swiss national flag, and, in reverse colors, the flag of the Red Cross; he also presided over the First Geneva Conference, which established the International Red Cross. Switzerland's highest mountain is named after him (Pointe Dufour).

Mazagrans were popular drinks in the cafés along the boulevards of Paris during the *Belle Époque*. The name of the drink recalls the heroism of the French forces in the Battle of Mazagran in Algeria in 1840. The different Mazagrans are named after generals and distinguish themselves by the use of different types of alcohol. To make a tasty Mazagran, it is important to use freshly prepared (and not cold) coffee. The recipe for *Mazagran à la Général Dufour* comes from Alessandro Filippini, one of the great chefs at Delmonico's in New York.

PARDO MULE

Fill half of a regular glass with crushed ice. Add 1 oz. of vodka and 3 dashes of passion fruit syrup and mix well. Add 3 oz. of ginger beer and mix gently to avoid decarbonizing the ginger beer. Serve with 4 lemon slices as garnish.

The Festival del film Locarno is one of Switzerland's most outstanding international cultural events. Since 1946, it has discovered new trends in the film industry and launched the careers of directors and actors. The festival's most impressive and unparalleled feature is the open-air screening on the Piazza Grande with up to 8,000 spectators. The festival's top prize is the Golden Leopard (pardo) awarded to the best film in the international competition.

The *Pardo Mule* is a refreshing drink served at the bar at the Festival del film Locarno.

RITZ FIZZ

Add 1 dash of Amaretto, 1 dash of Blue Curaçao and the juice of half a lemon to a shaker. Add ice to the shaker and shake until chilled. Strain into a champagne glass and top with chilled champagne. Add a rose petal as garnish.

The Ritz Fizz is one of the elegant champagne cocktails prepared at the bar of the London Ritz hotel.

ROBERT E. LEE COOLER

Mix the juice of half a lemon, 2 teaspoons of sugar, 2 oz. of gin, 2 oz. of club soda and one dash of absinthe well in a regular glass. Add ice to the glass and top with ginger ale. Garnish with a lemon twist and an orange spiral.

For a long time, Switzerland and the United States were the only republics on the globe, the so-called Sister Republics. The Swiss saw the Civil War as a struggle for the republic as a form of statehood. After the war, the Swiss government commissioned a mural on the American Civil War for the Swiss House of Parliament. The painter Frank Buchser never completed the painting, but he did important portraits of its main protagonists. Today the portraits of General Robert E. Lee and General William T. Sherman are in the Swiss Residence in Washington, D.C.

The *Robert E. Lee Cooler* recalls the drinks of the Old South. The recipe for it was published shortly after the end of Prohibition in *The Old Waldorf-Astoria Bar Book.*

SHERMAN

Add 1 oz. of sweet vermouth, 0.5 oz. of whiskey, 3 dashes of absinthe, 1 dash of Angostura bitters and one dash of orange bitters to a shaker. Add ice to the shaker and shake until chilled. Strain into a martini glass. Serve immediately with a lemon twist as garnish.

The Sherman is a strong short drink well suited to General Sherman's bold character. Like the recipe for the Robert E. Lee Cooler, this recipe was published in *The Old Waldorf-Astoria Bar Book.*

SMOKE ON THE WATER

Add 1.3 oz. of malt whiskey, 1 oz. of vanilla liqueur and 1 dash of lemon bitters to a shaker. Add ice to the shaker and shake until chilled. Strain into a martini glass. Serve immediately with fresh lemongrass as garnish.

Smoke on the Water is a song by the English rock band Deep Purple first released on their 1972 album *Machine Head.* The lyrics of the song tell a true story. On December 4, 1971, Deep Purple was in Montreux, Switzerland, where they rented their mobile studio at the Montreux Casino (in the song lyric "the gambling house") from the Rolling Stones. On the eve of the recording session, a Frank Zappa concert was held at the casino's theatre, the theatre's final concert before the casino complex closed down for the annual winter renovations. The place suddenly caught fire when someone in the audience fired a flare gun toward the rattan-covered ceiling ("some stupid with a flare gun"). There were no major injuries, but the fire destroyed the entire casino complex. The smoke on the water referred to the smoke from the fire spreading over Lake Geneva from the burning casino as seen by Deep Purple from their hotel. The "Funky Claude" running in and out is Claude Nobs, the founder and then director of the Montreux Jazz Festival who helped some of the audience members to escape from the fire. "Smoke on the Water" became an international hit, and Deep Purple formed a lasting bond with the town of Montreux. The song is honored by a sculpture along the lakeshore right next to the statue of Queen front man Freddie Mercury.

The *Smoke on the Water* cocktail was created by the Montreux Jazz Café.

ST. MORITZINO

Add 1 oz. of fresh lemon juice, 1 oz. of Cointreau, 1 oz. of vodka and 0.3 oz. of almond syrup to a shaker. Add ice to the shaker and shake until chilled. Strain into a martini glass.

St. Moritz is a high Alpine luxury resort in the Canton of Grisons, Switzerland. It is a popular destination for the upper class and international jet set with many luxurious five-star hotels. Badrutt's Palace is the most famous among them. On the shores of Lake St. Moritz, it looks like a fairy tale castle from far away with its landmark tower. Badrutt's was built in the late 19th century. The St. Moritz Winter Olympics in 1928 and 1948, the luxury of the hotel, and primarily the celebrities among the guests have made Badrutt's Palace a famous place. It was where Alfred Hitchcock stayed on his honeymoon and many times afterward, where personalities such as Henry Ford, the Duke and Duchess of Windsor, Marlene Dietrich, Greta Garbo, the Aga Khan, Joan Collins, Audrey Hepburn, Mel Ferrer, King Hussein of Jordan, Gunther Sachs, and Brigitte Bardot enjoyed themselves.

The *St. Moritzino* cocktail—a creation of Badrutt's Palace—makes us dream of that glamour.

SWISS DREAM

Add 0.6 oz. of cherry brandy, 0.6 oz. of Crème de cacao and 0.6 oz. of cream to a shaker. Add ice to the shaker and shake until chilled. Strain into a short glass.

Harry Schraemli (1904–1995) was a gifted bartender and the author of more than fifty culinary books. He ran the first American bar in Europe (Netherlands). Through training programs and his masterwork *Lehrbuch der Bar*, he introduced generations of Swiss bartenders to the art of mixology. Harry Schraemli created many cocktails with "Swiss" in their name.

The *Swiss Dream* cocktail is one of Harry Schraemli's original creations. The cacao and the cream might well be a reference to Switzerland as a hub for chocolate production and dairy products.

TELL'S SHOT

Add a few ice cubes, 3.3 oz. of apple juice, 1.5 oz. of grapefruit juice, 0.6 oz. of lemon juice, 0.6 oz. of grenadine and 0.6 oz. of almond syrup to a regular glass. Mix well and serve with an apple slice as garnish.

The best known episode in the Swiss national hero's life is when he is forced by the brutal *Landvogt* (bailiff) Gessler to shoot an apple from the head of his son Walter with his crossbow. It does not come as a surprise that the main ingredient in the *Tell's Shot* cocktail is apple juice.

ZÜRI-LEU

Add 0.6 oz. of vodka, 0.6 oz. of dry vermouth, 0.3 oz. of apricot brandy and 1.5 oz. of grapefruit juice to a shaker. Add ice to the shaker and shake until chilled. Strain into a champagne glass with an orange peel as garnish.

Züri-Leu is Swiss German and means Lion of Zurich. The lion is the heraldic animal of Zurich that replaced the imperial eagle around 1700. The heraldic change demonstrated that henceforth Zurich no longer derived its legitimacy from the emperor, but from its citizens. Today the lion is present everywhere in Zurich as a symbol of the city.

The *Züri-Leu* cocktail is attributed to Peter Roth, bartender at the Kronenhalle, who reportedly received a Golden Diploma for the drink at the 1977 Salon culinaire mondial.

IN SEARCH OF A
SWISS NATIONAL CUISINE

All those astonishing and dazzling careers, dishes, drinks and stories are sparkling crystals from culinary Switzerland. They lead back to fascinating times and awaken your eyes, nose and palate. But are those crystals also parts of a mosaic? Does an overall picture emerge from them? Is there Swiss cuisine comparable to French, Italian or Chinese cuisine?

The world's great cuisines have not only produced delicious dishes, they also have an unmistakable character. They have developed their own preparation methods and their own culinary terms; they have an unmistakable style with a high recognition value. In Switzerland, there is no such cuisine. The stories in this book cannot be assigned to any canon. Despite those culinary achievements and discoveries and the ingenuity of excellent chefs, why didn't great Swiss cuisine come to be?

That question has occupied me for a long time. I couldn't find a satisfactory answer either in books, magazines or on the Internet, or in the many conversations I had. In the end, I worked out my own explanation, which, though, is based on impressions rather than on close reasoning.

Cuisine and eating habits are an expression of political, economic, societal, and cultural conditions. That interconnection makes them exciting. To get a clear view of them, you have to remove yourself from the spell of the individual stories and recipes. We have to search for the picture that emerges from the crystals.

On the Internet, I came across a remarkable definition: "Swiss cuisine combines influences from German, French and Northern Italian cuisine. However, it is very varied from the regional standpoint, roughly divided up according to linguistic regions. Many dishes, though, have crossed local borders and are popular throughout Switzerland." Obviously it is even difficult for a definition trying very hard to be objective to describe the characteristic features of Swiss cuisine. It is determined by its influences and therefore remains rather unclear. Each attempt at classification seems to be foiled by deviations and exceptions. Yet that is precisely what hits the nail on the head.

Swiss cuisine's most well-known and most popular dishes originated a long time ago. They are characterized by areas and their inhabitants. Mountainous regions produced other dishes than the Mittelland; rural areas are not familiar with the same cuisine as the cities. The collection *Kulinarisches Erbe der Schweiz* (Culinary Heritage of Switzerland), but also most Swiss cookbooks are therefore consistently classified by cantons or regions. They often seem like finds from a trip to Switzerland. This variety is an overarching characteristic feature of Switzerland's culinary heritage. Although the regional cuisines can be inventoried and put together into collections, they do not amount to a national cuisine; in fact, that is because there is no main cultural center in the country and at the same time there is a great openness toward the larger cultural and linguistic areas of Europe with which Switzerland is closely connected to this day.

Although there was an aristocracy in the old Confederation and society was divided into classes, there was no royal court and no courtly life. The example of France shows that those elements were decisive in the emergence of French cuisine. At the court, there was not only enough money for select ingredients and trained staff, but above all there was the representative role with the corresponding social acceptance of and effect on the respective cuisine of the country, making it possible to establish a dining and cuisine culture.

Why is the connection between eating and social relations important? Eating has always been more than simply food intake; it is a social activity with many roles in group formation, social hierarchy, communication, and culture creation. In his study *The Civilizing Process*, Norbert Elias went into the different aspects of the communal meal. And he was only one—however an especially brilliant one—of the researchers of this phenomenon.

Many aspects shape the social structure of a dinner party. The seating arrangement is significant since you can guess a person's importance from it. The order in which the guests are served is meaningful since it reveals the hierarchy. Lower-ranking guests are served only after higher-ranking ones. Whether women sat at the table or ate in their own rooms, when they were served and whether they themselves were allowed to reach for the food said a great deal about their status. Eating and everything connected with it was an illustration of power relations.

With respect to cuisine, it is important that the quality of the dishes can also express social differences. In the Middle Ages, the cooking at courts was done (sometimes excessively) with precious spices. To keep a distance between the social classes, expensive ingredients such as truffles, duck liver, turtles, even flamingo tongues and other ingredients were used at sophisticated dinners in most eras, ingredients which were beyond the means of ordinary people. French haute cuisine, which predominated in Europe for a long time, clearly kept its distance from the cuisines below it. Haute cuisine, cuisine bourgeoise and cuisine régionale are a reflection of class society, important for distinction and identity.

Federal Switzerland, an entity made up of independent small states, did not strive for a center of power. The Diets of the old Confederation took place at changing locations; a central administration with a permanent seat did not come into being until the modern federal state was founded in 1848. To this day, Switzerland does not have a capital city (*Hauptstadt*), but only a federal city (*Bundesstadt*), that is, a seat of the important institutions of the Swiss Confederation.

The individual cantons and linguistic regions have kept their uniqueness as a result of that. Diversity and federalism have facilitated the relations with the other linguistic and cultural regions each time. Independent of its relationship with the European Union, Switzerland is a part of three larger European cultural areas. In that sense, the insistence on autonomy, diversity and regionalism is a guarantee for Switzerland as a cosmopolitan country.

Swiss cuisine is unmistakably a reflection of those political and cultural conditions: classified by diverse regions, but also always closely connected with the cuisines of the neighboring cultural areas. The fact that the most well-known culinary contributions were achieved abroad by no means diminishes the contribution of Swiss chefs, but emphasizes their persistence and organizational talent in addition to their specialized knowledge and their wealth of imagination. Maestro Martino, Vatel, Ritz, and Oscar of the Waldorf were masters who had an impressive international impact. Almost all of them stayed connected with their country of origin and their roots, creating dishes which recalled their homeland. Some chefs also suggested their homeland by the names they gave to individual dishes.

A Swiss national cuisine would be contrary to the essence and social reality of the country. Precisely because the practitioners of Swiss culinary art had to be limited by the absence of a national cuisine, they made an astonishing contribution to the culinary history of the world; and they have done so to this day.

LIST OF RECIPES

COLD HORS D'OEUVRES

Chocolate Foie Gras Mousse Truffles (Swiss Residence)   6

Endive, Watercress and Apple Salad (Delmonico's)   62

Mousseline de saumon (Dunand)   51

President Johnson's Chopped Garden Salad (Henry Haller)   97

President Reagan's Lobster Mousseline (Henry Haller)   98

Salade Irma (Ritz Hotel)   80

Waldorf Salad (Oscar of the Waldorf)   88

HOT HORS D'OEUVRES

Chocolate Fettuccini   9

Lobster Newberg (Delmonico's)   60

Omelette aux asperges / Aspargus Omelette (Vatel   41

Ravioli di Carne (Maestro Martino)   24

Vol au vent à la Béchamel (Joseph Favre)   71

Zucche Fritte (Maestro Martino)   22

FISH

Roasted Salomon (Anna Wecker)   33

MEAT DISHES

Chicken Waldorf Style (Oscar of the Waldorf)   89

Chocolate, Coffee, and Chipotle Braised Beef Short Ribs   11

Côtelettes à la Maintenon (Vatel)   42

Delmonico Steak 63

Gigot de mouton à l'italienne (Joseph Favre) 72

Involtini (Maestro Martino) 25

Poulet Marengo (Dunand) 52

President Ford's Chicken Cordon Bleu (Henry Haller) 100

Tournedos Rachel (Ritz Hotel) 82

SAVORY DISHES

Soufflé aux Morilles / Morel Soufflé (Vatel) 44

DESSERTS

Äpfelkrapfen mit Vanille Apfelmus / Apple Beignets with
  Vanilla Apple Purée (Anna Wecker) 34

Baba au Rhum (Delmonico's) 148

Baked Alaska (Delmonico's) 64

Cherry Pie (Maestro Martino) 146

Chocolate Lava Cake with Raspberry, Hot Chocolate
  Sauce and Whipped Cream (Swiss Residence) 14

Fraises à la Ritz 83

Glace au pomme Talleyrand-Périgord (Dunand) 53

Mrs. Nixon's Florida Lime Pie (Henry Haller) 102

Meringues, crème Chantilly et baies fraîches (Vatel) 45

Pan Rostito al Sapor di Fragole (Maestro Martino) 26

Salvator Pudding (Joseph Favre) 74

Toblerone Mousse 144

Cocktails and Drinks

MISCELLANEOUS

BIBLIOGRAPHY

Abad, Reynald. 'Aux origines du suicide de Vatel: les difficultés de l'approvisionnement en marée au temps de Louis XIV'. *Dixseptième siècle*. Société d'études du XVIIe siècle, no. 217. Paris 2002/4, pp. 631-641.

Andressen, Michael B. *Barocke Tafelfreuden an Europas Höfen.* Stuttgart, Zürich 1996.

Aulnoit, Béatrix de et Philippe Alexandre. *Des fourchettes dans les étoiles. Brève historie de la gastronomie française.* Paris 2010.

Bircher-Benner, Maximilian Oscar. *Die Grundlagen unserer Ernährung.* Berlin 1921.

Bircher, Ralph. *Leben und Lebenswerk Bircher-Benners.* Braunwald 2014.

Bräm, Urs. 'Kappeler Milchsuppe'. *Spuren - Horizonte.* Zürich 2011.

Branda, Pierre. *Napoléon et ses hommes: la Maison de l'Empereur 1804–1815.* Paris 2011.

Braudel, Fernand. *Civilisation matérielle, économie et capitalisme (XVe–XVIIIe siècles).* Paris 1979.

Chastonay, Adalbert. *Cäsar Ritz - Leben und Werk.* Visp 1994.

Choate, Judith and James Canora. *Dining at Delmonico's.* New York 2008.

Classen, Albrecht. *The Power of a Woman's Voice in Medieval and Early Modern Literatures.* Berlin 2007.

Dahinden, Martin and Anita Dahinden. *Dishes for the Generals' Room.* Washington, D.C., 2015.

Dahinden, Martin. 'Kulinarische Diplomatie und Schweizer Küchengeheimnisse'. *EIZ Band 189, Kellerhals (Hrsg.), Die*

Schweiz und Europa, Referate zur Fragen der Zukunft Europas 2017. Zürich 2018

Dahinden, Martin. *Schweizer Küchengeheimnisse: Gesichter und Geschichten hinter bekannten Gerichten*. Zürich 2016.

Dahinden, Martin. 'Switzerland's Culinary Footprint in the United States'. American Swiss Foundation Event. The Union League Club. New York, May 4th, 2016. http://www.foodinsight.org.

Dubois, Urbain et Émile Bernard. *Cuisine classique*. Paris 1856.

Dumas, Alexandre. *Grand dictionnaire de cuisine*. Paris 1873.

Dumont, Cédric. *Allegro con Gusto. Rezepte und Geschichten von komponierenden Feinschmeckern, kochenden Kapellmeistern und verwöhnten Primadonnen*. Bern 1982.

Dünnebier, Anna und Gert von Paczensky. *Kulturgeschichte des Essens und Trinkens*. München 1999.

Elias, Norbert. *Über den Prozess der Zivilisation. Soziogenetische und psychogenetische Untersuchungen*. Basel 1939, München 1969.

Escoffier, Auguste. *Le guide culinaire, aide-mémoire de cuisine pratique*. Paris 1903, 1921.

Escoffier, Auguste. *A Guide to Modern Cookery*. London 1907.

Favre, Joseph. *Dictionnaire universel de cuisine pratique*. Paris 1902.

Filippini, Alexander. *The Delmonico Cook Book*. New York 1880.

Filippini, Alexander. *The Table: How to Buy Food, How to Cook It, and How to Serve It*. New York 1888.

Filippini, Alexander. *The International Cook Book*. New York 1911.

Flandrin, Jean-Louis. *Tables d'hier, Tables d'ailleurs*. Paris 1999.

Fos, Léon de. *Gastronomiana*. Paris, Clermont-Ferrand 1870.

Friedell, Egon. *Kulturgeschichte der Neuzeit*. München 1927-1931.

Grandi, Ferdinando. *Les nouveautés de la gastronomie princière*. Paris 1866.

Harmon Jenkins, Nancy. 'Two Ways of Looking at Maestro Martino'. *Gastronomica: The Journal of Critical Food Studies*, Vol. 7/2, spring 2007, pp. 97-103.

Haver, Gianni. 'Dame à l'antique avec lance et bouclier: Helvetia et ses Déclinaisons'. *Hors-champs. Eclats du patrimoine culturel immatériel.* Neuchâtel 2013, pp. 274-282.

Kaiser, Dolf. *Fast ein Volk von Zuckerbäckern – Bündner Konditoren, Cafetiers und Hoteliers in europäischen Landen bis zum 2. Weltkrieg.* Zürich 1985.

Keller, Georg. *Die Hirsebreifahrt der Zürcher nach Strassburg 1576.* Zürich 1976.

Lagasse, Emeril. *Emeril's Delmonico. A Restaurant with a Past.* New York 2005.

Landau, Barry H. *The President's Table.* New York 2007.

Larousse Gastronomique. English Edition. London 1988.

Gaulis, Louis. *Pionniers suisses de l'hôtellerie.* Paudex 1976.

Haller, Henry. *The White House Family Cookbook. Two Decades of Recipes, a Dash of Reminiscence, and a Pinch of History from America's Most Famous Kitchen.* New York 1987.

Hundert Küchenspezialitäten aus allen Kantonen. Fabrik von Maggis Nahrungsmitteln in Kemptthal. Zürich o.J. (ca. 1940).

Knieriemen, Heinz: 'Bircher-Benner und sein Vermächtnis'. *Natürlich. Das Magazin für ganzheitliches Leben*, Nr. 7. Aarau 2003.

Das kulinarische Erbe der Schweiz. Online-Enzyklopädie der traditionellen Schweizer Küche. *www.patrimoineculinaire.ch.*

Lately, Thomas (Robert V. Steele). *Delmonico's. A Century of Splendor.* Boston 1967.

Laurioux, Bruno. 'Le prince des cuisiniers et le cuisinier des princes: nouveaux documents sur maestro Martino'. *Médiévales*, no. 49, pp. 141-154. Paris 2005.

Malortie, Ernst von. *Das Menu.* Hannover 1888.

Maestro Martino of Como. The Art of Cooking: The First Modern Cookery Book. California Studies in Food and Culture. 2005.

Mennel, Stephen: *All Manners of Food. Eating and Taste in England and France from the Middle Ages to the Present.* Oxford 1985.

Messerli Bollinger, Barbara E. 'Die bildliche Darstellung der Küche im Kochbuch der Anna Weckerin'. *Die Küche, wie sie im Buche steht. Ausstellung im Wohnmuseum Bärengasse.* Zürich 1989.

Müller, Peter. 'Oscar Tschirky'. *Historisches Lexikon der Schweiz. Stiftung Historisches Lexikon der Schweiz.* Basel 2002-2014.

Nicolardot, Louis: *Historie de la table.* Paris 1868.

The Oxford Companion to Food. Alain Davidson und Tom Janie. Oxford 2014.

Perrini, Giacomo. *Giacomo Perini's Schweizerzuckerbäcker oder genaue Unterweisung zur Anfertigung aller in der Konditorei vorkommenden Arbeiten insbesondere ...* Weimar 1893.

Perren, Beat H. *Jubiläumsschrift 150 Jahre Matterhorn.* Zermatt 2015.

Pfiffner, Albert. 'Julius Maggi'. *Historisches Lexikon der Schweiz.* Basel 2002-2014.

Piguet, Edgar. 'Schweizer in Italien'. *Schweizer im Ausland. Von ihrem Leben und Wirken in aller Welt.* Neue Helvetische Gesellschaft und Auslandschweizer-Kommission. Genf 1931.

Pivot, Monique. *Maggi et la magie du bouillon Kub.* Paris 2001.

Quinzio, Jeri und Geraldine M. *Of Sugar and Snow. A History of Ice Cream Making.* Oakland 2010.

Ranhofer, Charles. *The Epicurean.* New York 1894.

Revel, Jean-François. *Un festin en paroles: historie littéraire de la sensibilité gastronomique de l'Antiquité à nos jours.* Paris 2007.

Riley, Gillian. *Painters and Food. Renaissance Recipes.* San Francisco 1993.

Ritz, Marie-Louise. *César Ritz - Host to the World.* Paris 1981.

Rossfeld, Roman. *Schweizer Schokolade. Industrielle Produktion und kulturelle Konstruktion eines nationalen Symbols 1860–1920.* Baden (Schweiz) 2007.

Roulet, Claude. *Ritz, une histoire plus belle que la légende.* Paris 1998.

Schäfer, Hermann. ,Julius Maggi'. *Neue Deutsche Biographie,* Band 15. Berlin 1987.

Schraemli, Harry. *Das grosse Lehrbuch der Bar.* 4. Auflage. Luzern 1949.

Schraemli, Harry. *Der Meistermixer. Ein Taschen-Lexikon für Berufsmixer und deren Mitarbeiter mit über 1500 delikaten Rezepten.* Luzern 1961.

Schraemli, Harry. *Von Lukullus zu Escoffier. Geschichte der Feinschmeckerei.* Bielefeld o.J.

Schriftgiesser, Karl. *Oscar of the Waldorf.* New York 1943.

Schweizer Armee Reglement 60.006: Kochrezepte. Bern 2009

Tannahill, Reay. *Food in History.* London, New York 1988.

Trefzer, Rudolf. *Klassiker der Kochkunst. Die fünfzehn wichtigsten Rezeptbücher aus acht Jahrhunderten.* Zürich 2009.

Tschirky, Oscar. *The Cook Book by ,Oscar' of the Waldorf.* Chicago und New York 1896.

Weber, J. J. *Universal-Lexikon der Kochkunst.* 6. Auflage. Leipzig 1897.

Wairy, Louis Constant. *Mémoires de Constant, premier valet de chambre de l'Empereur, sur la vie privée de Napoléon, sa famille et sa cour.* Paris 1830.

Wecker, Anna. *Ein köstlich new Kochbuch.* Amberg 1598. Reprint. München 1977.

Wirz, Albert. *Die Moral auf dem Teller. Dargestellt an Leben und Werk von Max Bircher Benner und John Harvey Kellogg.* Zürich 1993.

Wolff, Eberhard (Hrsg.). *Lebendige Kraft: Max Bircher-Benner und sein Sanatorium im historischen Kontext.* Baden (Schweiz) 2010.

Zieman, Hugo and F. L. Gilleth. *The White House Cook Book.* New York, Akron, Chicago 1913.

Zimmermann, Pedro. *Tafelfreuden. Köstliche Geschichten aus der Schweiz.* Zürich 1993.

CPSIA information can be obtained
at www.ICGtesting.com
Printed in the USA
BVHW03*0905110618
518748BV00012B/276/P

9 781632 636317